WALKING THE FOOL'S PATH

A TAROT MAP TO THE SOUL

ARWIN VALENCIA, MD

First Edition – Printed in the United States of America

To the Seeker within us all

*The dreamer who dares to step into the
unknown, the wanderer who listens for
whispers of destiny, and the soul who knows
that every ending is but a beginning.*

Walking the Fool's Path

Upon the edge where silence sings,
The Fool steps forth with open wings.
A leap of faith, the heart made whole,
He seeks the lantern of the soul.

The Magician calls with hands of flame,
To shape the world, to give it name.
The High Priestess, cloaked in night,
Reveals the hidden, veils of sight.

The Empress blooms with life's embrace,
Creation's rhythm, nature's grace.
The Emperor stands, a mountain tall,
With order's voice to guide us all.

Through Lovers' vows and Chariot's might,
Through Strength that tames the shadow's fight,
The Hermit's lamp, the Wheel's command,
All weave the map the cards have planned.

The Tower falls, the Star shines clear,
The Moon reflects both hope and fear.
The Sun then rises, bright and true,
Awakening joy in all we do.

Completion comes, the World at last,
Yet circles turn, no path is past.
The Fool steps on—forever whole
Walking the Tarot, map of soul.

Table of Contents

Introduction

The Fool's First Step

Upon the edge, the Fool stands tall,
Hearing the inner whisper's call.
A mirror shines, both dark and bright,
Revealing shadows, birthing light.

No map, no chains, no fate to bind,
Just open heart and seeking mind.
Each step unknown, yet wholly true,
The path begins, and so do you.

The Tarot as a Mirror of the Soul

For centuries, the Tarot has been cloaked in mystery, often misunderstood as a fortune-teller's tool, a mystical mechanism for predicting what is yet to come. But its deepest wisdom does not lie in forecasting an uncertain future. Instead, Tarot functions as a mirror of the soul: a sacred book of images and symbols that reflect back to us what already resides within.

The seventy-eight cards, and especially the twenty-two of the Major Arcana, speak in a symbolic language older than words. Their imagery reaches into the hidden caverns of the psyche, illuminating subconscious patterns, forgotten dreams, and untapped potential. When we look into the Tarot, we are not peering outward into destiny, we are gazing inward into the timeless landscape of the Self.

The Fool: Archetype of Beginning

At the heart of this mirror stands the Fool. Numbered zero, belonging both everywhere and nowhere, the Fool is the eternal traveler who takes the first step into the unknown. With a light satchel slung over the shoulder, a faithful companion at their feet, and eyes lifted toward the horizon, the Fool embodies innocence, openness, and limitless possibility.

This archetype is not "foolishness" in the worldly sense. Rather, it is a sacred naïveté—a radical trust in life itself. The Fool teaches us that all true journeys of transformation begin with surrender: the willingness to risk, to leap without certainty, to be reshaped by what we do not yet know. To live the Fool's archetype is to awaken to life as an adventure of becoming, a process where even missteps hold meaning and every fall becomes initiation.

A Universal Language of Wisdom

The Tarot's power lies in its capacity to bridge worlds—spiritual and psychological, mystical and practical, ancient and modern. Each card is layered with meaning:

- **Numerology** speaks through the vibration of numbers, tracing cycles of creation and completion.
- **Astrology** weaves planetary energies and zodiacal rhythms into the archetypes.
- **Mythology and mysticism** echo through timeless stories and divine figures.
- **Psychology**, especially Jung's insights, reveals Tarot as a map of the collective unconscious.

Together, these dimensions create a symbolic ecosystem, a living text that evolves with us. Tarot is not a closed book; it is an open dialogue. Its messages shift as we shift, offering guidance not by dictating outcomes but by unveiling what stirs within us at each stage of the path.

Tarot and the Inner Journey

Modern psychology validates what mystics have long known: the journey of the soul is also the journey of integration. Carl Jung described individuation as the process of becoming whole—of reconciling shadow and light, persona and essence, conscious and unconscious. The Tarot, filled with archetypal figures, offers a visual pathway for this process.

When we engage with the cards, we are not simply interpreting images; we are encountering aspects of ourselves. Each spread becomes a dialogue with the unconscious, each card a mirror of inner truth. The Fool's leap into the unknown is also our own leap into self-discovery, where synchronicity—those meaningful coincidences Jung described—guides us toward greater awareness

Walking the Fool's Path

This book is an invitation to walk that path with intention. Each chapter will take you deeper into the Major Arcana, exploring not only the historical and symbolic meaning of each card but also its psychological, spiritual, and practical dimensions. You will discover how archetypes link to astrology and numerology, how myths weave into our personal stories, and how the cards can serve as companions for meditation, reflection, and inner transformation.

Practical exercises, journaling prompts, and contemplative practices will be offered to ground these insights into daily life. In this way, Tarot becomes more than theory or symbol, it becomes a lived experience, a mirror you return to again and again, each time seeing yourself anew.

The First Step

The Tarot does not exist to dictate your fate or forecast distant tomorrows. Its wisdom lives in the present moment. It reveals the patterns, possibilities, and invitations already at play within you, waiting for your recognition.

And so, we return to the Fool, standing at the cliff's edge, unburdened by certainty, carrying only the faith that the path itself will unfold. In this archetype we see not only the Fool of Tarot, but also ourselves—ever on the threshold of a new beginning.

The journey toward self-knowledge, toward wholeness, begins as all great journeys do: with a single, courageous step.

This book is that step. This is your path.

ARWIN VALENCIA, MD

Part I

The Framework of the Journey

Chapter 1

Tarot as a Spiritual Map

Introduction: A Deck of Mystery and Meaning

At first glance, a deck of Tarot cards looks like nothing more than an artfully designed pack of cards, adorned with mysterious images of kings, queens, magicians, hermits, and wheel-like mandalas. To the uninitiated, it might seem like a curious relic, an antique plaything, or even something to be dismissed as superstition. Yet beneath the surface lies a profound spiritual map, one that has been quietly guiding seekers for centuries. Tarot, in its essence, is not simply a fortune-telling device. It is a symbolic language, a mirror of the soul, and a chart of consciousness.

The Tarot has traversed centuries and cultures, transforming from a 15th-century game of aristocrats into one of the most potent tools for psychological exploration and spiritual awakening. Its journey mirrors our own: playful beginnings that evolve into deep questioning, trials, revelations, and ultimately, the search for wholeness.

The Origins of Tarot

15th-Century Italy: Cards of Nobility

The first Tarot decks emerged in Northern Italy during the mid-15th century, with the **Visconti-Sforza deck** being among the earliest and most elaborate. These cards were hand-painted masterpieces, created for noble families who enjoyed them as part of a game called *tarocchi*. Much like the modern game of bridge, *tarocchi* was a game of triumphs, played with wit, competition, and strategy. At this stage, Tarot had no overtly mystical associations—it was an art form and pastime for the elite.

Possible Roots in the Islamic World

Some scholars trace Tarot's structural origins to the **Mamluk deck** of the Islamic world, which contained suits resembling swords, cups, and coins. These designs, when carried into Europe, may have seeded the development of the Tarot's suits—later known as Wands, Cups, Swords, and Pentacles. Thus, Tarot carries within it the cross-cultural exchange between East and West, play and symbol, art and mysticism.

From Game to Esoteric Symbolism

The Occult Revival of the 18th & 19th Centuries

It was not until the **18th century** that Tarot stepped beyond entertainment into the realm of esotericism. French occultist **Antoine Court de Gébelin** published writings that claimed the Tarot contained remnants of ancient Egyptian wisdom, hidden in its trump cards. Though historically inaccurate, his theory captivated imaginations. Suddenly, the Tarot was not merely a game—it was a book of wisdom disguised in images.

Linking Tarot to Mystical Traditions

Later occultists connected the Tarot to **Kabbalah, alchemy,** and **Hermeticism,** weaving it into the rich tapestry of Western mysticism. The 19th-century secret society known as the **Hermetic Order of the Golden Dawn** gave Tarot the systemization it retains today. Members of the Golden Dawn—such as A.E. Waite and Aleister Crowley—saw in Tarot a coded spiritual system. They aligned the cards with astrology, the Tree of Life, and magical rituals, transforming Tarot into a full symbolic language of the soul.

The Symbolic Language of Tarot

The Major Arcana: Archetypes of the Journey

At the heart of Tarot lie the **22 cards of the Major Arcana,** each depicting a universal archetype: The Fool, The Magician, The High Priestess, The Lovers, Death, The World, and so on. These images are not random; they represent stages of life, patterns of consciousness, and spiritual truths. They are *maps of being,* showing the spectrum of experience from innocence to mastery, from ignorance to enlightenment.

The Minor Arcana: The Elements of Daily Life

Complementing the Majors are the **56 Minor Arcana,** arranged into four suits:

- **Wands (Fire)** – creativity, willpower, inspiration.
- **Cups (Water)** – emotions, relationships, intuition.
- **Swords (Air)** – intellect, conflict, clarity.
- **Pentacles (Earth)** – material life, body, work, stability.

These suits reflect the four elements of classical philosophy and the four dimensions of human existence. Together, the Majors and Minors form a complete symbolic map of both the extraordinary and the ordinary, the eternal and the everyday.

The Fool's Journey: A Spiritual Blueprint

The Story Unfolds

One of the most powerful ways to understand Tarot is through the **Fool's Journey,** a narrative that follows the Major Arcana sequentially from card 0 (The Fool) to card 21 (The World). The Fool, representing innocence and potential, steps into the unknown, beginning a path of discovery. Along the way, he meets teachers, allies, challenges, and revelations.

- With The Magician and High Priestess, he learns about the balance of conscious will and hidden intuition.
- With The Lovers, he encounters the tension of choice and relationship.
- With Death, he confronts transformation and the necessity of letting go.
- At last, with The World, he achieves a sense of completion and integration.

This journey is more than allegory. It mirrors the cycles of growth in every human life—the losses, the loves, the awakenings, and the triumphs.

Jungian Psychology and Archetypes

Swiss psychologist **Carl Jung** observed that myths, dreams, and symbols often repeat across cultures. He called these recurring figures **archetypes**; universal patterns rooted in the collective unconscious. The Tarot's Major Arcana, with its archetypes of The Mother (Empress), The Father (Emperor), The Wise Old Man (Hermit), and Death, resonates deeply with Jungian psychology. Tarot thus becomes a bridge between ancient symbolism and modern psychology, helping individuals access unconscious wisdom.

Tarot as a Mirror of the Soul

The Subconscious Connection

Tarot is not about predicting a fated future—it is about reflecting the inner state of the seeker. When cards are laid out in a spread, the images evoke unconscious associations. The **subconscious mind**, which often communicates in symbols and dreams, finds in Tarot a mirror. Through this mirror, hidden truths rise into awareness.

A Path to Wholeness

Working with Tarot can lead to what Jung called **individuation**, the process of integrating all aspects of the self into wholeness. The shadow, the inner child, the anima/animus, the hero—all these psychic forces appear in Tarot's imagery, waiting to be acknowledged and integrated. By dialoguing with the cards, one begins a dialogue with the soul.

Archetypal Path of Evolution

Tarot and the Hero's Journey

Comparisons between Tarot and **Joseph Campbell's Hero's Journey** are frequent. Just as the hero sets out, faces trials, meets mentors, and returns transformed, so too does the Fool progress through triumphs and trials toward completion. Each Tarot archetype embodies a step in the timeless cycle of departure, initiation, and return.

Collective and Personal Story

On one level, the Tarot speaks to **collective human experience**—the inevitability of change, the necessity of love, the power of transformation. On another level, it speaks to **personal narrative**—the unique ways these universal truths manifest in an individual's life. This duality makes Tarot both universal and intimate.

Tarot as Personal Narrative

Storytelling with the Cards

When someone reads Tarot, they are not passively receiving a fortune; they are actively engaging in storytelling. The images become prompts, and the querent projects their life story into them. This act of projection is not mere imagination—it is a revelation of inner truths. By reframing challenges in symbolic form, individuals gain perspective, resilience, and meaning.

Healing Through Symbol

Because Tarot externalizes inner struggles into images, it can be profoundly therapeutic. A person wrestling with loss may see Death not as an end, but as transformation. A person feeling stuck may see The Hanged Man and recognize the wisdom of surrender. In this way, Tarot facilitates healing, helping individuals reshape their personal narratives into ones of growth and empowerment.

Bridging Traditions: Tarot as a Spiritual Map

A Meeting of Mysticism, Psychology, and Spirituality

Tarot is unique in that it bridges multiple dimensions:

- Mysticism – its ties to Hermeticism, Kabbalah, and esoteric traditions.
- Psychology – its resonance with Jungian archetypes and symbolic language.
- Spirituality – its ability to guide seekers toward self-realization, mindfulness, and union with the divine.

Tarot does not demand blind belief, it invites contemplation. It does not dictate destiny—it illuminates possibility. It is not rigid dogma—it is fluid imagery, ever-shifting to meet the seeker where they are.

The Tarot as a Compass for the Soul

To walk with the Tarot is to walk with a compass, not a map set in stone. It points toward directions of growth, highlighting where one may find clarity, balance, or shadow. The Major Arcana represent the landmarks of transformation, the Minor Arcana, the everyday terrain.

Together, they form a **sacred cartography of the human soul.**

Conclusion: Walking the Path with Tarot

Tarot, born as a game, has matured into one of the most enduring spiritual maps available to humanity. From Renaissance courts to occult circles, from Jungian analysts to modern seekers, its images continue to reveal layers of meaning.

To hold a Tarot deck is to hold a mirror of the human journey: the laughter of The Fool, the stern wisdom of The Hermit, the transformative fire of Death, and the wholeness of The World. It is a tool of reflection, meditation, and awakening, guiding seekers not to an external fate, but to an internal truth.

As we proceed deeper into this book, each chapter will explore the Major Arcana as stages of this spiritual map. The Fool's step will become our step, and the journey of the archetypes will illuminate our own. In this way, Tarot is not just studied, it is *lived*.

Practical Applications: Walking the Map Yourself

Tarot becomes most transformative not when studied abstractly, but when lived experientially. The cards invite us into dialogue with ourselves. Each image opens a doorway into the subconscious and, through reflection, helps us align more consciously with our spiritual path.

Below are suggested practices—journaling prompts, reflective questions, and guided meditations—that can help you, the seeker, engage directly with the symbolic power of Tarot as a spiritual map.

Journaling Prompts

Take a quiet moment, shuffle your deck (if you have one), or simply contemplate the ideas below. Write freely, without censoring yourself. The purpose is to access hidden insights.

1. **The Map of My Soul:**

- If my life were a Tarot card right now, which one would it be?

- What does its symbolism reveal about my current stage in the journey?

2. **The Fool's First Step:**

- Where in my life am I being asked to take a leap of faith, to step into the unknown?

- What fears or hesitations hold me back from stepping fully into this new beginning?

3. **Major vs. Minor Lessons:**

- Reflect on a recent experience. Was it a *Major Arcana* moment (transformative, life-shifting) or a *Minor Arcana* one (ordinary, everyday learning)?

- How can I honor both the extraordinary and the ordinary in my journey?

4. **Archetypes in My Life:**

- Who in my life plays the role of *The Magician* (mentor, creator, catalyst)?

- Who embodies *The High Priestess* (keeper of secrets, intuition, inner wisdom)?

- How do these archetypes live within me?

5. **Reframing Challenges:**

- Think of a recent difficulty. If it were a Tarot card, which one would it be?

- How does seeing it through this archetypal lens shift my perspective?

Guided Meditation: Entering the Fool's Path

This meditation will help you connect personally with the Tarot as a living spiritual map.

1. **Preparation:**

   Sit comfortably, close your eyes, and take three deep breaths.

Imagine yourself holding a Tarot deck in your hands.

2. **The Fool Appears:**

> Visualize the card of **The Fool**. See the youthful traveler, standing at the edge of a cliff, a small bag over his shoulder, a dog at his side.

- Notice his open heart, his trust in the unknown, his joy.

3. **The Invitation:**

- Imagine The Fool turning toward you, offering you a flower or extending his hand.

- Ask yourself silently: *Where in my life am I being invited to begin again?*

4. **Walking the Path:**

- See a winding road stretching out before you, lined with the images of the other 21 Major Arcana cards.

- Begin to walk with The Fool, sensing that each card holds a lesson you will one day encounter.

5. **Integration:**

- When you are ready, thank The Fool for his guidance.

- Return slowly to the present moment, opening your eyes with a deeper awareness of your own journey.

Daily Practice: Tarot as a Mirror

For those who wish to weave Tarot into their daily spiritual practice, consider the following exercise:

- **Morning Card Pull:** Draw one card each morning. Instead of asking "What will happen today?" ask:

What aspect of my inner world is this card reflecting?

- Spend 5 minutes journaling about how the card's symbolism might serve as guidance for your thoughts, emotions, or choices that day.

Over time, this practice cultivates mindfulness, teaching you to see life through the layered wisdom of archetypes and symbols.

Closing Reflection

Tarot, as you have seen in this chapter, is more than a system of fortune-telling. It is a **spiritual cartography of the human experience**, a dialogue between the conscious and unconscious, a living myth that continues to unfold in your own life.

The Major Arcana provides the landmarks of evolution; the Minor Arcana anchors the lessons of daily living. Together, they create a mirror that reflects both your personal story and the universal patterns of the soul.

As you step forward into the next chapters, remember: **You are The Fool.** Every shuffle, every spread, every card you draw is an echo of your journey toward wholeness. The Tarot does not hand you answers—it hands you yourself.

Chapter 2

Astrology and the Tarot

Major Arcana Astrology

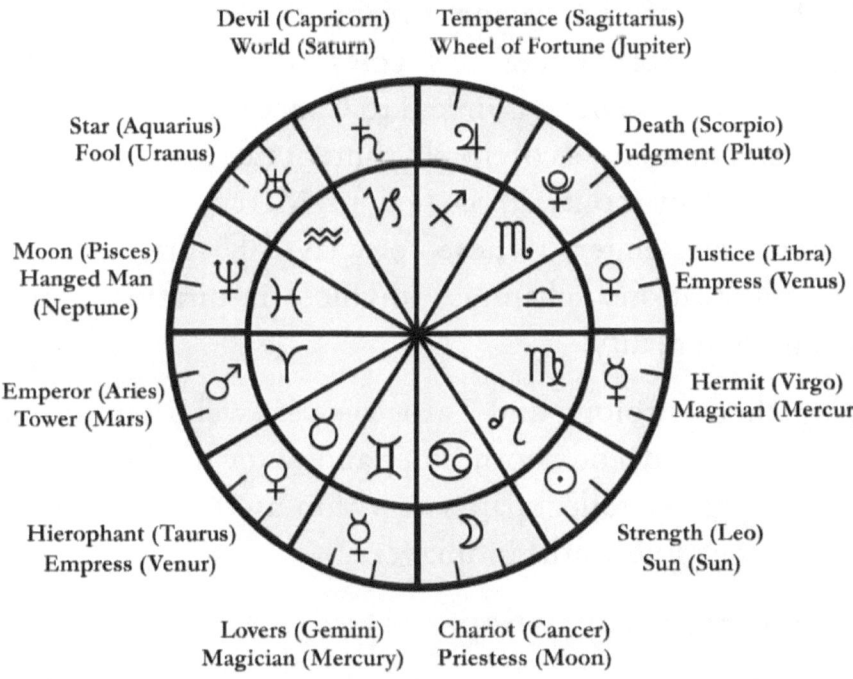

Figure 1 - Astrology of the Major Arcana

Tarot as a Cosmic Mirror

The Tarot, while often approached as a divinatory tool, is also a **cosmic mirror**—a system where the archetypes of the Major Arcana align with astrological energies, planetary influences, and the cyclical patterns of existence. Through these connections, Tarot becomes not only a symbolic map of the psyche but also a spiritual calendar of the cosmos.

Each card of the Major Arcana carries not just an archetypal story but also a **celestial resonance**. The Chariot, for instance, is linked to Cancer and the Moon's cycles, reminding us of the rhythms of tide and time. The Magician, by contrast, is tied to Mercury, the fleet-footed messenger, whose powers of intellect and communication channel divine inspiration into manifested reality.

Together, astrology and Tarot weave a web of meaning that helps us decode both inner and outer worlds. Just as the stars above reflect patterns within us, the cards below reveal the same truths in imagery.

Zodiac Sign Associations

The Major Arcana's symbolism has long been mapped onto the **twelve zodiac signs**, where the essence of each sign aligns with a card's archetypal role:

- Aries: The Emperor — authority, initiative, leadership.

- Taurus: The Hierophant — tradition, stability, sacred order.

- Gemini: The Lovers — duality, choice, relationship.

- Cancer: The Chariot — willpower, protection, navigation of emotional tides.

- Leo: Strength — courage, vitality, radiant self-expression.

- Virgo: The Hermit — introspection, wisdom, analysis.

- Libra: Justice — balance, fairness, discernment.

- Scorpio: Death — transformation, endings, rebirth.

- Sagittarius: Temperance — expansion, integration, higher wisdom.

- Capricorn: The Devil — material tests, limitations, mastery of shadow.

- Aquarius: The Star — hope, vision, collective destiny.

- Pisces: The Moon — mystery, intuition, dream states.

These associations remind us that the Tarot reflects the same archetypal energies that astrology charts across the heavens.

Planetary Associations

Beyond the zodiac signs, the planets themselves are mapped onto the Major Arcana, deepening their esoteric resonance:

- Uranus: The Fool — sudden awakening, leaps into the unknown.
- Mercury: The Magician — communication, intellect, transformative speech.
- Moon: The High Priestess — intuition, hidden wisdom, the subconscious.
- Venus: The Empress — fertility, love, beauty, abundance.
- Sun: The Sun — vitality, clarity, radiant joy.
- Mars: The Tower — upheaval, force, radical liberation.
- Jupiter: Wheel of Fortune — expansion, luck, cycles of destiny.

- Saturn: The World — structure, completion, mastery of cycles.
- Neptune: The Hanged Man — surrender, mystical vision, transcendence.
- Pluto: Judgment — transformation, resurrection, reckoning.

In this system, the cosmos becomes a Tarot deck in motion: Uranus pushes us to leap, Mercury teaches us to speak and craft, the Moon pulls us toward dreams, and Saturn ensures the cycle completes.

Astrology of the Minor Arcana

The **Minor Arcana** reflects the flow of everyday life— our thoughts, choices, relationships, and material concerns. Unlike the Major Arcana, which signify archetypal, transformative forces, the Minor Arcana show how these energies manifest in practical, short-term ways. Astrology provides a rich interpretive framework for the Minor Arcana by linking the **36 numbered cards (2 through 10 in each suit)** to the **36 astrological decans** (10° subdivisions of the zodiac).

This system (commonly used in Hermetic traditions like the Golden Dawn) allows each card to carry not only elemental meaning (fire, water, air, earth) but also planetary rulership and zodiac flavor, offering specificity and depth.

The Four Suits and the Elements

- **Wands → Fire (Aries, Leo, Sagittarius)**
  Passion, creativity, vitality, ambition, and willpower.

- **Cups → Water (Cancer, Scorpio, Pisces)**
  Emotion, intuition, relationships, dreams, and receptivity.

- **Swords → Air (Gemini, Libra, Aquarius)**
  Intellect, analysis, communication, conflict, and clarity.

- **Pentacles → Earth (Taurus, Virgo, Capricorn)**
  Materiality, work, health, stability, prosperity, and grounded-ness.

Each suit expresses the flow of its element through numbers, beginning with pure potential (Ace) and ending in completion or transition (Ten).

Decans, Modalities, and Numbered Cards

The zodiac is divided into **12 signs**, each 30° long. These are further divided into **three 10° sections** called **decans**, each ruled by a different planet.

- **Cardinal signs (Aries, Cancer, Libra, Capricorn):** Initiative, beginnings, leadership.

- **Fixed signs (Taurus, Leo, Scorpio, Aquarius):** Stability, endurance, power.

- **Mutable signs (Gemini, Virgo, Sagittarius, Pisces):** Flexibility, change, transition.

The Minor Arcana's numbered cards (2–10) map directly onto these decans:

- 2, 3, 4 = Cardinal signs
- 5, 6, 7 = Fixed signs
- 8, 9, 10 = Mutable signs

This gives each card a specific zodiac sign and planetary ruler.

Suit by Suit Breakdown

Wands (Fire Signs)

- **2 of Wands (Mars in Aries):** Bold vision, decisive beginnings.

- **3 of Wands (Sun in Aries):** Expansion, foresight, manifestation.

- **4 of Wands (Venus in Aries):** Harmony, celebration, union.

- **5 of Wands (Saturn in Leo):** Struggle, competition, ego clashes.

- **6 of Wands (Jupiter in Leo):** Triumph, leadership, recognition.

- **7 of Wands (Mars in Leo):** Defense, resilience, standing ground.

- **8 of Wands (Mercury in Sagittarius):** Swift change, messages, movement.

- **9 of Wands (Moon in Sagittarius):** Persistence, inner strength, vigilance.

- **10 of Wands (Saturn in Sagittarius):** Burden, responsibility, overextension.

Cups (Water Signs)

- **2 of Cups (Venus in Cancer):** Love, connection, union.

- **3 of Cups (Mercury in Cancer):** Friendship, celebration, joy.

- **4 of Cups (Moon in Cancer):** Withdrawal, contemplation, emotional apathy.

- **5 of Cups (Mars in Scorpio):** Loss, grief, emotional challenge.

- **6 of Cups (Sun in Scorpio):** Nostalgia, innocence, past influences.

- **7 of Cups (Venus in Scorpio):** Illusion, choices, fantasy.

- **8 of Cups (Saturn in Pisces):** Letting go, walking away, seeking deeper truth.

- **9 of Cups (Jupiter in Pisces):** Wish fulfillment, satisfaction, abundance.

- **10 of Cups (Mars in Pisces):** Harmony, family, spiritual joy.

Swords (Air Signs)

- **2 of Swords (Moon in Libra):** Indecision, balance, denial.

- **3 of Swords (Saturn in Libra):** Heartbreak, sorrow, painful clarity.

- **4 of Swords (Jupiter in Libra):** Rest, retreat, recovery.

- **5 of Swords (Venus in Aquarius):** Discord, manipulation, hollow victory.

- **6 of Swords (Mercury in Aquarius):** Transition, healing journey, new perspective.

- **7 of Swords (Moon in Aquarius):** Deception, strategy, hidden motives.

- **8 of Swords (Jupiter in Gemini):** Restriction, paralysis, trapped thought patterns.

- **9 of Swords (Mars in Gemini):** Anxiety, nightmares, inner torment.

- **10 of Swords (Sun in Gemini):** Ending, painful closure, surrender.

Pentacles (Earth Signs)

- **2 of Pentacles (Jupiter in Capricorn):** Balance, adaptability, resource juggling.

- **3 of Pentacles (Mars in Capricorn):** Teamwork, mastery, collaboration.

- **4 of Pentacles (Sun in Capricorn):** Security, possession, control.

- **5 of Pentacles (Mercury in Taurus):** Poverty, loss, spiritual hardship.

- **6 of Pentacles (Moon in Taurus):** Generosity, giving and receiving, balance.

- **7 of Pentacles (Saturn in Taurus):** Patience, long-term investment, delayed harvest.

- **8 of Pentacles (Sun in Virgo):** Skill, craftsmanship, self-mastery.

- **9 of Pentacles (Venus in Virgo):**
  Refinement, luxury, independence.

- **10 of Pentacles (Mercury in Virgo):**
  Legacy, wealth, family continuity.

Astrological Correspondences of the Minor Arcana

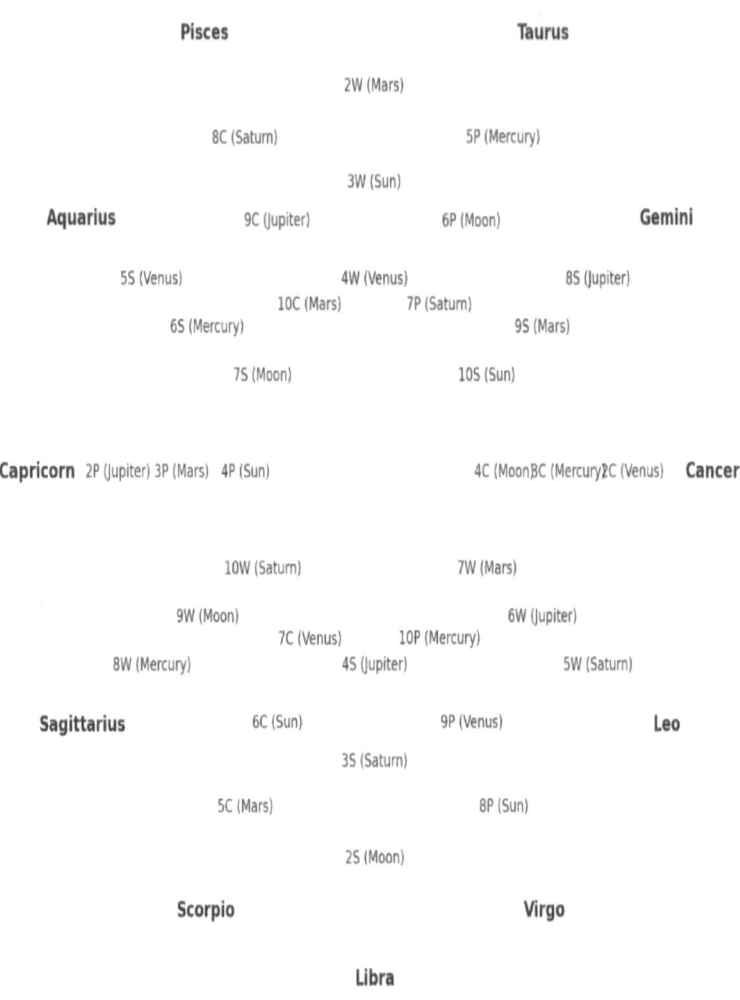

Figure 2 Minor Arcana decan correspondences

How It Applies in Readings

When a Minor Arcana card appears:

1. **Suit = Elemental energy** (Fire, Water, Air, Earth).

2. **Number = Zodiac sign & modality** (e.g., fixed water = Scorpio).

3. **Planetary ruler of the decan = Flavor and detail** (e.g., Mars in Scorpio = intensity, struggle → 5 of Cups).

This allows you to read the card not just as "general energy" but as a **precise astrological snapshot** of how that energy plays out in daily life.

In practice:

- Pulling the **6 of Wands** isn't just "victory"—it's *Jupiter in Leo*, expansive recognition, leadership affirmed, a time when one's talents shine brightly.

- The **9 of Swords** is not simply "anxiety"—it is *Mars in Gemini*, mental overdrive, scattered battles, a war fought in the mind.

Thus, the Minor Arcana becomes a **microcosm of astrological energy**, grounding the archetypal themes of the Major Arcana into daily experiences.

The Fool's Journey as Cosmic Pilgrimage

The Fool's Journey—Tarot's archetypal storyline—can be understood as a **cosmic pilgrimage**. The Fool, stepping into the unknown, mirrors the soul embarking on incarnation. Each card thereafter represents encounters with cosmic forces—archetypes that teach, test, and transform.

- Embarking into the Unknown: The Fool leaps, as the soul does, into the mystery of life.

- Encounters with Archetypes: The Magician, the Empress, the Wheel of Fortune—each a force or lesson shaping growth.

- Transformation and Growth: Through Death, the Devil, and the Tower, the soul meets challenge and shadow.

- Integration: The World marks the return to wholeness, where the soul gather.

Case Study: The Chariot & The Magician

Themes: Willpower, Cycles, and the Power of Communication

Background

The Chariot (Cancer / Moon cycles) and the Magician (Mercury / communication) represent a potent pairing:

one governs **emotional navigation**, the other governs **mental articulation**. Where the Chariot provides direction through tides of feeling, the Magician translates vision into action through precise communication.

Their combined energy speaks to **mastery of self and expression**—the ability to ride emotional currents while using language, thought, and intention as instruments of creation.

Scenario: Navigating a Life Transition

Subject: Maya, 32, professional writer

- Recently promoted to a leadership role in publishing.

- Feels overwhelmed by responsibility and fluctuating emotions.

- Wants to embrace authority without losing empathy.

The Chariot (Cancer / Moon Cycles)

The Moon rules Cancer, and its phases affect Maya's rhythm. She notices bursts of creativity at the waxing moon, clarity at the full, and retreat at the waning. These cycles mirror the **Chariot's dual sphinxes**—opposing forces requiring mastery.

- **Challenge:** Avoiding burnout by resisting lunar tides.

- **Practice:** Moon journaling to honor cycles and plan work accordingly.

- **Lesson:** Mastery comes from harmonizing inner tides, not suppressing them.

The Magician (Mercury / Communication)

Mercury's influence highlights Maya's role as communicator. The Magician teaches her to treat words as spells and speech as alchemy. In meetings, she practices deliberate pauses, affirmations, and intentional phrasing.

- **Challenge:** Translating intuitive insights into clear leadership.

- **Practice:** Using affirmations, rehearsed clarity, and precise speech.

- **Lesson:** Words are tools—when wielded consciously, they shape collective reality.

Astrology Deepens the Tarot

Tarot symbolism, though rooted in archetypes, becomes more alive when **anchored in the heavens**. Astrology is the moving sky; Tarot is its symbolic mirror. Planets, signs, and cycles amplify the archetypes of the Major Arcana, giving us not just meaning but timing.

The Chariot (Cancer, Moon cycles) and the Magician (Mercury

Act I: Mercury Retrograde — The Magician's Shadow

Three months into her leadership role, Mercury entered retrograde. Maya dismissed the warnings— "I don't believe in cosmic excuses," she told herself. But the Magician archetype had a lesson waiting.

At a critical editorial meeting, Maya presented a new strategy for digital publications. She spoke with passion but hurried through details. Unbeknownst to her, an email she sent earlier contained a typo in the budget figures. Her team misinterpreted the numbers, and soon confusion spread. One colleague accused her of "pushing unrealistic expectations."

Maya felt her chest tighten. She was the Magician, but her wand faltered—her words, once meant to inspire, had become distorted spells.

That evening, reflecting in her journal, she wrote:

"Mercury retrograde feels like a mirror turned inward. My communication must not only inspire but also clarify. Precision is love."

Lesson: Mercury retrograde taught her to slow down, double-check, and refine. She began printing her notes before meetings, rehearsing aloud, and using pauses to emphasize clarity. She learned that the Magician's true power is not in dazzling performance but in **measured truth**.

Act II: Cancer Lunar Eclipse — The Chariot's Trial

Six weeks later, under a Cancer lunar eclipse, the Chariot's energy surged. At work, a sudden restructuring unsettled the team. Long-time employees worried about job security, and fear spread like a tide.

Maya herself felt raw, as though old childhood insecurities had resurfaced. She wanted to retreat, to hide. Yet, the Chariot appeared—asking her to hold the reins even as emotional waves crashed.

At a late-night team meeting, the tension broke. One editor burst into tears, voicing fears of being "discarded." The room grew heavy with silence. Maya felt the eclipse inside her—darkness swallowing her composure.

But then she remembered the dual sphinxes of the Chariot: one black, one white. Emotion and reason. Retreat and courage. She steadied her breath, placed her palms on the table, and said:

"I can't promise what the company will decide tomorrow. But I can promise this: we are a team. I will advocate for each of you, and together we'll steer this ship through."

The room softened. Tears turned into nods. Maya realized the Chariot's victory isn't about suppressing emotion but **guiding it with steadiness.**

Lesson: The eclipse illuminated her role as both shield and driver. Emotional honesty, when coupled with calm leadership, became her chariot's armor.

Act III: Interplay: When Retrogrades Meet Eclipses

At times, a Mercury retrograde overlaps with a lunar eclipse. This is where the Magician and Chariot collide—communication and emotional mastery must dance under cosmic tension.

- If Maya reacts emotionally (Chariot unbalanced), her words (Magician) scatter and confuse.

- If she communicates rashly (Magician unchecked), she destabilizes herself and others emotionally (Chariot).

- But when she pauses to observe the tides (Moon) and then chooses her words carefully (Mercury alchemy), she turns cosmic challenge into spiritual victory.

These intersections show us that astrology does not dictate fate but reveals **testing grounds—moments when the archetypes demand conscious embodiment.**

Reflective Practices – Journaling Prompts

1. What "opposing sphinxes" pull at you emotionally, and how might you guide them toward one direction?

2. What recent Mercury retrograde experience revealed patterns in how you communicate under stress?

3. How have lunar eclipses or full moons unearthed emotions you could no longer ignore?

4. When have your words (Magician) either calmed or inflamed emotions (Chariot) in yourself or others?

Ritual: Eclipse & Retrograde Alignment

- On the night of a lunar eclipse, sit under the moonlight.

- Place two candles before you: one silver (Moon/Chariot) and one yellow (Mercury/Magician).

- Write two lists:

- Emotional patterns you're ready to release (Chariot work).

- Communication habits you wish to refine (Magician work).

- Burn the lists, releasing them to the eclipse and retrograde energies.

Speak aloud an affirmation:

"I master my tides; I master my words; I create harmony through balance."

Guided Meditation: Steering Through Cosmic Crossroads

1. Imagine yourself in a chariot beneath a sky where the moon is eclipsed. Darkness and light swirl across its surface.

2. You feel the pull of two sphinxes—one emotional, one rational. Hold the reins gently, steadying your breath.

3. Ahead, Mercury appears as the Magician, holding a staff of light. He reminds you that your words are wands, your thoughts incantations.

4. As you guide the sphinxes forward, speak within:

"I ride the tides without fear. I choose words of clarity and truth. My heart and voice move as one."

Final Reflection

The Chariot and the Magician teach us that astrology is not distant fate but **living practice.** Lunar eclipses test whether we can hold emotional reins; Mercury retrogrades test whether we can wield words wisely. Together, they form a curriculum of **soul mastery— emotional intelligence married to verbal alchemy.**

To walk the Fool's Path here is to learn this:

- The Moon cycles remind us of rhythm and receptivity.

- Mercury retrogrades remind us of reflection and precision.

- The integration of both creates a leader, healer, and creator aligned with   cosmic law.

Maya's story reminds us that astrology and Tarot are not abstract—they unfold in our lives daily. When Mercury retrogrades, the Magician asks us to refine our speech. When the Moon eclipses in Cancer, the Chariot asks us to hold steady. Together, they teach us the sacred art of living the cycles as **initiations of the soul.**

Chapter 3

Numerology and the Tarot

Introduction: The Language of Numbers in the Tarot

Numbers are more than symbols of quantity; they are the architecture of creation. From the harmony of Pythagoras' music of the spheres to the mystical calculations of Kabbalah, numbers have been regarded as archetypal forces—patterns that describe not only how the universe is structured but also how the soul evolves.

Numerology, the study of number symbolism, acts as a sacred lens through which we decode meaning. Numbers embody vibration, rhythm, and progression, offering insight into both cosmic law and personal transformation. When applied to Tarot, they reveal hidden layers of order behind the apparent randomness of shuffled cards.

The Tarot itself is constructed on a numerological foundation. The **Major Arcana**, numbered 0 through 21, traces the archetypal journey of the Fool, mirroring the spiral of growth, death, and rebirth. The **Minor Arcana**, with suits numbered from Ace (1) to Ten, depicts the everyday lessons that mirror these archetypes in ordinary life. Together, Tarot and numerology form a system of sacred mathematics—one that charts the eternal dance of spirit and matter.

To understand Tarot deeply is to see that the cards are not isolated pictures but parts of a numerical code. The Fool's zero, the Magician's one, the Hermit's nine, and the World's twenty-one are not arbitrary markers but stages in the soul's pilgrimage. The wisdom of numerology ensures that the Fool's Journey is not only symbolic but vibrationally aligned with the universal order.

Section I: Numbers 0–9 – The Foundation of Spiritual Growth

0 – The Fool: Infinite Potential

Zero is paradox itself. It is emptiness and fullness, absence and infinity. In mathematics, zero allows for all calculations; in mysticism, it is the cosmic void—the womb of creation. In Tarot, the Fool embodies zero, symbolizing the soul unformed, stepping into incarnation with innocence, trust, and infinite potential.

Journaling Prompts:

- Where in my life am I being asked to take a leap of faith?

- How does embracing uncertainty open new doors for me?

Guided Meditation:

Visualize yourself standing on the edge of a cliff with the open sky before you. As you step forward, you feel carried by unseen hands. Whisper: *I trust the unknown. I am infinite possibility.*

1 – The Magician: Initiation and Manifestation

One is the spark, the singularity, the focused will. It marks the birth of individuality. The Magician channels energy from above to below, symbolizing the power of intentional creation.

Journaling Prompts:

- What resources and talents do I already have to create the life I desire?

- How can I use focused intention to manifest change?

Guided Meditation:

See yourself at a table with the four elements before you. Raise your hands as light pours through you into each tool. Affirm: *I am a conduit of creation. My will shapes my reality.*

2 – The High Priestess: Duality and Intuition

Two introduces polarity—day and night, conscious and unconscious, seen and unseen. The High Priestess teaches that truth is not always rational but revealed through inner knowing.

Journaling Prompts:

- What inner knowing have I been ignoring?
- How can I deepen my relationship with my intuition?

Guided Meditation:

Imagine sitting before a veiled temple. Inside, the High Priestess hands you a scroll. Place it against your heart, knowing the answers reside within you.

3 – The Empress: Creativity and Growth

Three is expansion, fertility, and creativity. The Empress nurtures beauty, growth, and abundance.

Journaling Prompts:

- How am I nurturing myself and others?
- What creative projects or ideas am I ready to birth?

Guided Meditation:

Walk through a lush garden of endless abundance. Place your hands on your heart, breathing in green light. Whisper: *I am a vessel of beauty, love, and growth.*

4 – The Emperor: Structure and Stability

Four is solidity, foundation, and order. Represented by the Emperor, it reflects authority, boundaries, and discipline.

Journaling Prompts:

- Where in my life do I need more structure?

- How do boundaries protect my well-being?

Guided Meditation:

See yourself within a stone fortress. Each wall represents strength, safety, and clarity. Stand tall and affirm *I am grounded, stable, and sovereign.*

5 – The Hierophant: Tradition and Transformation

Five signifies change and growth through challenge. The Hierophant channels this into spiritual learning, showing how to balance tradition and innovation.

Journaling Prompts:

- Which teachings or traditions serve me and which do I need to release?

- Where am I called to be a teacher or a student?

Guided Meditation:

Picture yourself in a sacred temple. A wise teacher places their hand on your head, filling you with timeless wisdom. Whisper: *I receive wisdom. I embody wisdom.*

6 – The Lovers: Harmony and Choice

Six is balance restored, now enriched with awareness. The Lovers embody choice, reflecting how union with others mirrors inner alignment.

Journaling Prompts:

- What choices align me with my higher self?
- How can I bring harmony into my relationships?

Guided Meditation:

Visualize yourself at a crossroads. Choose the path of love and step forward with your higher self-beside you. Affirm: *Love guides my choices.*

7 – The Chariot: Mastery and Determination

Seven represents discipline, testing, and focus. The Chariot symbolizes the mastery needed to harness opposing forces.

Journaling Prompts:

- Where do I need greater discipline to move forward?

- What forces in my life must I bring into balance?

Guided Meditation:

Imagine riding a chariot pulled by two sphinxes. Hold the reins steady as you move forward with confidence. Whisper: *I direct my destiny with focus and strength.*

8 – Strength: Power and Inner Mastery

Eight symbolizes infinity and balance. True strength is found in compassion and patience.

Journaling Prompts:

- How can I transform fear into courage?

- Where in my life can I embody compassion as strength?

Guided Meditation:

Approach a lion with calmness. Place your hand on its head as it bows in trust. Whisper: *My strength is born of love.*

9 – The Hermit: Completion and Wisdom

Nine is culmination, solitude, and harvest of wisdom. The Hermit carries the lantern of truth.

Journaling Prompts:

- Where do I need solitude to reflect?

- What wisdom am I ready to share from my own journey?

Guided Meditation:

See yourself holding a lantern atop a mountain at night. Its glow lights your path and inspires others behind you. Affirm: *My inner light guides the way.*

Section II: Numbers 10–21 – Expansion and Transformation

10 – Wheel of Fortune: Cycles and Destiny

- **Prompts:** What life cycle am I repeating? How can I surrender to change as destiny?

- **Meditation:** See a great cosmic wheel spinning, carrying you through both rise and fall. Whisper: *I flow with the rhythm of life.*

11 – Justice: Truth and Balance

- **Prompts:** What truth must I face right now? Where do I need to restore balance?

- **Meditation:** Visualize a scale balancing your heart and mind. Whisper: *I live in alignment with truth.*

12 – The Hanged Man: Surrender and Perspective

- **Prompts:** Where in my life do I need to release control? What new perspective is waiting for me?

- **Meditation:** Imagine yourself suspended upside down yet serene. Affirm: *Through surrender, I see clearly.*

13 – Death: Transformation and Renewal

- **Prompts:** What am I ready to let go of? How do endings in my life create new beginnings?

- **Meditation:** Walk through a forest of falling leaves. Whisper: *I release to be reborn.*

14 – Temperance: Integration and Harmony

- **Prompts:** Where am I being asked to find balance? What opposites in my life can I integrate?

- **Meditation:** Visualize two streams of water flowing into one golden cup. Whisper: *I am harmony. I am balance.*

15 – The Devil: Shadow and Liberation

- **Prompts:** What attachments or illusions are holding me back? How can I reclaim my freedom?

- **Meditation:** Imagine chains falling from your wrists as you rise into the light. Whisper: *I am free from illusion.*

16 – The Tower: Collapse and Awakening

- **Prompts:** What false structures in my life are ready to fall? How can I embrace upheaval as growth?

- **Meditation:** Visualize lightning striking a tower. As it crumbles, feel yourself released into new possibility. Whisper: *I am reborn in truth.*

17 – The Star: Hope and Renewal

- **Prompts:** Where am I being asked to restore faith? What dream lights my path forward?

- **Meditation:** Stand under a star-filled sky. Let one radiant star pour healing light into you. Whisper: *I am guided. I am renewed.*

18 – The Moon: Illusion and Intuition

- **Prompts:** What fears or illusions cloud my vision? How can I deepen trust in my intuition?

- **Meditation:** Walk a moonlit path between shadowy towers. Listen to your inner voice. Whisper: *I trust the wisdom of my soul.*

19 – The Sun: Joy and Illumination

- **Prompts:** Where in my life am I experiencing joy? How can I embrace more playfulness and vitality?

- **Meditation:** Picture yourself as a child riding a white horse under a brilliant sun. Whisper: *I shine with joy and light.*

20 – Judgment: Awakening and Renewal

- **Prompts:** Where in my life am I being called to rise to a higher purpose? What old patterns am I ready to release?

- **Meditation:** Hear a trumpet calling you to awaken. Rise renewed, leaving behind the past. Whisper: *I awaken to my highest self.*

21 – The World: Fulfillment and Wholeness

- **Prompts:** What cycle in my life feels complete? How am I embodying integration and wholeness?

- **Meditation:** See yourself dancing in a circle of light, embraced by all four elements. Whisper: *I am whole. I am complete.*

Section III: Master Numbers in Tarot

- **11 – Justice (Illumination & Clarity):**

Prompt: Where must I embrace truth without compromise?

Meditation: Visualize yourself glowing with white light that cuts through illusion.

- **22 – The World (Master Builder):**

Prompt: What vision of mine is ready to be built?

Meditation: Imagine laying stones of light into a temple of your destiny.

- **33 – The Empress Elevated (Sacred Service):**

Prompt: How can I serve the world with love?

Meditation: Hold the earth in your arms, sending it unconditional care.

Section IV: The Sacred Philosophy of Zero

Zero is the great mystery: emptiness that is fullness, nothing that contains everything. It frames the Fool's journey, reminding us that from nothing all things arise, and to nothing they return.

Traditions interpret zero as:

- **Shunyata (Buddhism):** Emptiness as infinite potential.

- **Ein Sof (Kabbalah):** The limitless before creation.

- **Tao (Taoism):** The void that gives birth to the ten thousand things.

Zero is the cosmic circle, the womb of all numbers, reminding us that beginnings and endings are illusions. Only the eternal cycle remains.

Prompt: Where in my life do I resist the void, and how might I embrace it as possibility?

Meditation: Sit in stillness, surrounded by infinite space. Dissolve into the circle of light. Whisper: *I am the void. I am the whole.*

Section V: Numerology in the Minor Arcana

The Minor Arcana translates these universal archetypes into daily life. Each suit expresses the numbers 1–10 through its elemental realm:

- **Wands (Fire):** Creativity and action.
- **Cups (Water):** Emotion and relationships.
- **Swords (Air):** Intellect and conflict.
- **Pentacles (Earth):** Material life and work.

The numerical sequence (Ace to Ten) reflects a full cycle of human experience:

- **Aces:** Seeds of potential.
- **Twos:** Duality and choice.
- **Threes:** Expansion and creativity.
- **Fours:** Structure and rest.
- **Fives:** Conflict and change.
- **Sixes:** Harmony restored.
- **Sevens:** Testing and challenge.
- **Eights:** Transformation and strength.
- **Nines:** Culmination.
- **Tens:** Completion and renewal.

Thus, the Minor Arcana is not random storytelling but a mirror of the numerological order within daily life.

The journey is not linear but spiral. Endings lead to beginnings; every World card opens into another Fool's leap. This reflects reincarnation, seasonal rhythms, and the eternal return.

Section VII: Numerology, Kabbalah, and the Tree of Life

In Kabbalistic mysticism, numbers correspond to the **ten sephiroth** on the Tree of Life, stages of divine manifestation from infinite source (Keter) to physical reality (Malkuth). The 22 paths between them correspond to the 22 Major Arcana, making Tarot a living diagram of the soul's ascent.

The numerology of Tarot thus aligns with Jewish mysticism, Hermetic philosophy, and Jungian depth psychology—making it not just a deck of cards, but a **multi-dimensional map of consciousness.**

Conclusion: Navigating Life with Numerological Insight

Numerology in Tarot is more than an intellectual tool— it is a compass of the soul. The numbers whisper that every ending is a beginning, every challenge a teacher, every cycle a return to wholeness.

By meditating on these numbers, seekers can identify patterns in their own lives, whether the resilience of the eight, the wisdom of the nine, or the fulfillment of the twenty-one. Tarot numerology becomes a sacred mathematics of the soul, reminding us that life is not random but ordered by archetypal rhythm.

Through numbers, the Fool's path becomes our path: a spiral journey through creation, dissolution, and rebirth, until we too learn to dance in the circle of zero, whole and infinite.

Chapter 4

Archetypes and the Psyche

Introduction: The Universal Language of Symbols

Humanity has always sought to understand the invisible forces shaping life. From the myths of ancient Greece to the sacred texts of the East, from folklore sung around campfires to the images painted in medieval cathedrals, symbolic stories have served as mirrors of the soul. They remind us that our experiences, though deeply personal, are also profoundly universal. Carl Jung, the Swiss psychologist and pioneer of analytical psychology, named this reservoir of shared meaning the **collective unconscious**. Within it reside **archetypes**—primordial images and patterns of behavior that echo across cultures and times.

The Tarot, with its vivid imagery and layered symbolism, can be seen as a living archive of these archetypes. Each card is not merely a picture but an invitation into the psyche, a way of contacting these universal energies and applying them to our personal journey. To walk the Fool's Path is to enter into dialogue with these inner figures, learning their lessons and integrating their wisdom into the unfolding story of our lives.

1. The Collective Unconscious: A Shared Inner World

Jung distinguished between the **personal unconscious**—our unique storehouse of repressed memories, forgotten experiences, and unresolved conflicts—and the **collective unconscious**, a deeper layer that belongs to humanity as a whole. Unlike the personal unconscious, the collective unconscious is not acquired through individual experience. Instead, it is inherited, much like the instinctual behaviors seen in animals.

This shared reservoir contains archetypes: timeless images that form the blueprint of human behavior and meaning. Just as every human body carries a genetic code, every human psyche carries symbolic imprints that express themselves through dreams, myths, rituals, and stories.

Examples abound:

- Flood myths appear in Sumerian, Hindu, Hebrew, and Mayan traditions.
- Heroic figures like Gilgamesh, Hercules, and King Arthur carry remarkably similar themes of trials, death, and rebirth.

- Mother goddesses—from Isis of Egypt to Demeter of Greece—embody nurture and fertility.

The collective unconscious connects us to this timeless tapestry. It explains why we feel resonance when encountering certain stories or symbols—they awaken something already within us.

2. Archetypes: The Universal Patterns of the Psyche

Archetypes are not rigid characters but dynamic energies, influencing both our inner life and our outer behavior. Jung described them as "forms without content" that become visible when clothed in cultural expression—myths, religious symbols, literature, and dreams.

Some of the primary archetypes include:

- **The Persona:** The mask we wear to interact with society. It protects the inner self but can also trap us if we mistake the mask for our true identity.

- **The Anima/Animus:** The inner contrasexual figure—the anima as the feminine within a man, the animus as the masculine within a woman. They represent our capacity to relate, create, and balance inner polarity.

63

- **The Shadow**: The unacknowledged, repressed, or denied aspects of the self. While often feared, the shadow holds tremendous creative energy when integrated.

- The Self: The archetype of wholeness, representing the union of conscious and unconscious elements of the psyche. It is the guiding principle of individuation.

- The Wise Old Man/Woman: A figure of inner guidance, wisdom, and mentorship.

- The Hero: Embodying courage, resilience, and transformation, the hero confronts trials and emerges renewed.

- The Trickster: Mischievous, chaotic, and boundary-breaking, the trickster destabilizes rigid systems, forcing growth through disruption.

These archetypes do not remain static. They emerge in dreams, project themselves onto others, or reveal themselves in symbolic encounters. For example, a strict boss might activate our perception of "The Father" archetype, while a creative muse may awaken the anima.

Archetypes act as organizing principles that shape the narrative of our lives.

3. Archetypes in the Tarot

The Tarot is a visual map of the archetypal psyche. Each Major Arcana card represents not just a symbolic scene but an archetype in motion.

- **The Magician**: The power of will, focused intention, and manifestation.
- **The High Priestess**: The anima as guardian of intuition and hidden wisdom.
- **The Devil**: The Shadow, representing attachment, illusion, and repressed desire.
- **The World**: The Self, the integration of opposites into wholeness.

In this way, Tarot and Jungian psychology share a language. Archetypes live in both systems, and engaging with Tarot offers us a way of dialoguing with these deep psychic forces.

4. The Collective Unconscious in Daily Life

While archetypes may seem abstract, their influence permeates daily experience:

- **Dreams**: A dream of being chased by a dark figure often represents the shadow archetype urging acknowledgment.

- **Relationships**: Romantic attraction often projects the anima or animus onto a partner, coloring the intensity of love and conflict.
- **Culture**: Films like *Star Wars* or *The Matrix* captivate because they retell the universal hero's journey.

Recognizing these patterns allows us to move from unconscious reaction to conscious engagement. Instead of being swept away by the archetype, we can learn from it.

5. Individuation: The Path to Wholeness

For Jung, the purpose of life was not merely adaptation to society but the pursuit of **individuation**—the integration of the conscious and unconscious into a harmonious whole. Individuation is not about perfection but about authenticity, living in alignment with one's true Self.

This process involves:

- Encountering the Shadow: Acknowledging repressed aspects and transforming them.
- Integrating the Anima/Animus: Embracing the inner opposite to achieve psychic balance.

- Transcending the Persona: Releasing identification with masks to discover the authentic Self.
- Union with the Self: Achieving a state where inner opposites harmonize and a deeper center of meaning emerges.

6. The Fool's Journey as Individuation

The Tarot's **Fool's Journey** mirrors the process of individuation.

- **The Fool (0):** Innocence, potential, and the leap into life.
- **The Magician & High Priestess:** Conscious will and unconscious wisdom, initiating polarity.
- **The Lovers:** Choice and integration of duality.
- **The Death Card:** Ego dissolution, the embrace of transformation.
- **The Star, Moon, and Sun:** Stages of healing, illusion, and illumination.
- **The World:** Completion, integration, and wholeness.

Each encounter along the Fool's spiral path invites us to confront an archetype, integrate its lesson, and move closer to the Self. This journey is never finished;

individuation unfolds throughout life, deepening as we age and experience new cycles.

7. Tarot as a Mirror of the Psyche

When we lay Tarot cards before us, we are not simply shuffling cardboard; we are activating the symbolic imagination. The cards speak the language of the unconscious, bypassing rational defenses to touch hidden truths.

Tarot facilitates:

- Shadow Work: Facing denied parts of the self, as when The Devil or The Tower appear.
- Self-Reflection: Recognizing patterns mirrored by the cards.
- Archetypal Connection: Experiencing universal energies—The Hero, The Wise Guide, The Trickster—within our personal journey.
- Intuition Development: Trusting inner wisdom as the cards resonate with our own symbolic associations.

By engaging with Tarot archetypes consciously, we bring unconscious material into awareness, advancing individuation.

8. Applications in Spirituality, Art, and Healing

Jung's archetypes have influenced diverse fields:

- **Spirituality**: Archetypes frame sacred figures like Christ (the Self), Mary (the mother), or Krishna (the Divine Child).
- **Art**: Literature and cinema continually recycle archetypal narratives, from Odysseus to Frodo Baggins.
- **Healing**: Jungian therapy employs dreams, myths, and symbols to uncover unconscious material and guide personal growth.
- **Tarot Practice**: As a psychological tool, Tarot provides a symbolic mirror for counseling, journaling, and meditation.

In all these contexts, archetypes function as bridges between the inner and outer worlds, enabling transformation.

9. Challenges and Critiques

While Jung's ideas remain influential, they have faced critiques:

- Some argue archetypes are cultural, not universal.
- Others find the collective unconscious difficult to prove scientifically.

- Tarot, likewise, is often dismissed as superstition.

Yet the enduring power of archetypes and symbolic imagery suggests that, whether literal or metaphorical, they hold truth. Myths, dreams, and Tarot readings continue to awaken insight and guide lives.

10. Conclusion: Embracing the Archetypal Journey

To understand archetypes is to recognize that our personal story is part of a larger human story. Each joy and sorrow, victory and loss, reflects an ancient rhythm. Through Jung's psychology and the Tarot's imagery, we come to see that life itself is mythic.

The Fool's Journey is our journey. With every step, we encounter the archetypes within: the shadow we fear, the lover we long for, the hero we become, and the Self we seek. Tarot becomes a mirror in which the psyche beholds itself—sometimes fragmented, sometimes whole, but always in motion toward integration.

By engaging consciously with archetypes, we are invited into a deeper relationship with ourselves and with life itself. This is the essence of individuation: not to escape the world, but to live it more fully, in harmony with the symbols that whisper through dreams, stories, and cards alike.

Guided Journaling Prompts

1. **Meeting Your Shadow**

   - Recall a recent situation where you felt triggered, defensive, or ashamed.

   - Ask yourself: *What hidden part of me is being reflected here?*

   - Write about how this "shadow" might actually carry unacknowledged strengths.

2. **The Archetypes in My Life**

   - List three people who have strongly influenced you (positively or negatively).

   - Identify which archetypes they represent (Hero, Wise Guide, Trickster, etc.).

   - Reflect: *What lessons have these figures awakened in me?*

3. **Persona vs. True Self**

   - Describe the "mask" you wear in your professional or social life.

   - How does it differ from how you feel inside?

   - Where do you long for greater authenticity?

4.   **Dialoguing with the Anima/Animus**

- If you are male, imagine your inner feminine (Anima) speaking to you.

- If female, imagine your inner masculine (Animus).

- Write a dialogue where this inner figure gives you guidance on balancing your life.

5.   **The Fool's Journey as Your Journey**

- Choose one Major Arcana card that resonates with your current life stage.

- Journal about how its imagery and archetype reflect your present challenges, lessons, and opportunities.

Ask: *What is this card inviting me to integrate right now?*

Guided Meditation Practices

1. Archetype Encounter Visualization

- Sit comfortably, breathe deeply, and imagine yourself walking a spiral path.

- Ahead, a figure approaches—an archetype you need to meet (it could be The Magician, The Shadow, The Mother, etc.).

- Allow the figure to speak. Listen without judgment.

- When the message is complete, bow in gratitude and slowly return.

- Journal about the encounter immediately afterward.

2. Tarot as Mirror Meditation

- Shuffle your Tarot deck in silence.

- Draw a single Major Arcana card and place it before you.

- Gaze at the image, breathing slowly, as if the card were a mirror of your psyche.

- Ask inwardly: *What part of me is this card reflecting today?*

- Close with three deep breaths and record your reflections.

3. Shadow Integration Breathwork

- Inhale: visualize drawing your repressed or denied emotions up to the surface.

- Hold: acknowledge them without judgment.

- Exhale: imagine releasing fear and resistance, allowing these energies to transform into strength.

- Repeat for 5–10 minutes.

4. Wholeness Alignment

- Visualize the four archetypes within you: Persona (mask), Shadow (hidden self), Anima/Animus (inner opposite), and Self (center of wholeness).

- See them seated in a circle, conversing in harmony.

- Allow the Self, the archetype of unity, to radiate light that integrates the others.

- Sit in this light until you feel centered and whole.

5. The Fool's Path Journey

- Imagine yourself as The Fool standing at the cliff's edge.
- Ahead, a spiral of 22 glowing gates stretches into the distance. Each gate is marked by a Major Arcana card.
- Walk through the gate that calls to you most strongly.
- Ask: *What lesson does this stage of my journey hold?*
- Absorb the wisdom, then return.

Closing Reflection

Working with archetypes is not an intellectual exercise but a living relationship. Through journaling and meditation, you allow these forces to move from abstract ideas into direct experience. The Tarot becomes not only a symbolic map but also a spiritual practice—one that leads you toward individuation and wholeness.

Part II: The Major Arcana Walking the Fool's Path

Chapter 5
The Fool: New Beginning

In the Tarot, **The Fool**, traditionally numbered 0, marks both the beginning and the infinite potential of a journey. Zero is not a void, but a seed—pregnant with possibility, untouched by form or limitation. The Fool stands at the threshold of experience, embodying the innocence, spontaneity, and courage required to leap into the unknown. This archetype asks us to trust not in what is seen, but in what is felt—our intuition, our inner compass—and to take that first step even when the destination remains unclear.

The Fool is not reckless, but *fearless in faith*. He invites us to shed our preconceptions and embrace the unfolding mystery of life. He represents a moment suspended in time—a sacred pause before the plunge—where anything is possible and everything is yet to be defined.

Symbolism and Spiritual Meaning

A Fresh Start and Limitless Potential:

The Fool signals the start of a new chapter, a blank page in the book of life. It might arise during a time of transition, or when a leap of faith is being called for—whether in career, relationships, spiritual evolution, or personal identity. It encourages us to move beyond comfort zones and familiar patterns and to engage life with curiosity, courage, and an open heart.

Trusting the Journey:

To walk the path of The Fool is to move with a quiet assurance that the universe will meet each step with synchronicity and support. It's not about being certain of the outcome but being open to the process. The Fool teaches that every misstep contains wisdom, and every detour, a hidden blessing.

Numerology and Astrology

In Tarot, *The Fool* (card 0) symbolizes new beginnings, infinite potential, and embracing the unknown. The number 0 reflects wholeness and limitless possibilities. Astrologically, The Fool is linked to **Uranus**, the planet of change and unpredictability, aligning with its adventurous nature. It's also loosely associated with **Pisces** for its imaginative and intuitive qualities, and with the **Air element**, representing freedom, insight, and movement.

The Fool in Jungian Psychology

In Jungian terms, **The Fool represents the archetype of the "Unrealized Self"**—the raw psychic potential that exists prior to conditioning, societal roles, or ego identity. He is the *original Self*, uncarved and unclaimed, setting forth on the great journey of individuation: the process of becoming whole by integrating the unconscious into the conscious self.

- ## The Unconscious Potential:

The Fool is not truly "foolish," but rather untouched by societal constraints. He represents the beginning of self-awareness, when the psyche begins its dance with shadow, symbol, and integration.

- ## Innocence as Strength:

Unlike cynicism masquerading as wisdom, the Fool's naivety allows him to perceive the world with fresh eyes. His innocence is reminiscent of the inner child—open to wonder, unafraid to stumble, eager to play. It is a spiritual reminder that wisdom is not merely knowledge, but the rediscovery of simplicity through experience.

- ## The Hero's Journey Begins:

Just as the Fool ventures through the twenty-one cards of the Major Arcana, so too do we traverse life's phases—each card a symbol of an inner threshold crossed, a shadow faced, or a truth reclaimed. The Fool becomes the *Hero*, not through grand acts, but through persistence, trust, and transformation.

- ## The Trickster Aspect:

The Fool also wears the mask of the **Trickster**, disrupting norms and exposing illusions. As such, he challenges us to question authority, redefine truth, and confront the false masks we wear. In this role, the Fool becomes a mirror—mocking rigidity and calling forth liberation.

Leaping into the Unknown

The Fool's leap from the cliff—often depicted in classic Tarot imagery—is symbolic of spiritual surrender. It's not recklessness, but *radical trust* in the unfolding of life. That moment of stepping into the unknown, without a map or a safety net, is where magic begins. The white rose he often carries is a symbol of purity and higher calling, and the small bundle over his shoulder reminds us that we already possess all we need.

We all face these moments—times when logic alone cannot guide us, and intuition whispers, "Leap." The Fool reminds us that the greatest transformations come not from clinging, but from releasing.

A Reflection of Our Own Journey

Whether we recognize it or not, every soul at some point awakens to the deeper call of self-discovery. What begins as an external quest—seeking purpose, love, or meaning—eventually reveals itself as an **inner journey**. Along this path, we encounter joys and heartbreaks, victories and failures. These are not signs of folly, but rites of passage.

As we evolve, The Fool is gradually transformed into other archetypes—The Magician, The Hermit, The

Lovers, The World—but his spirit remains. He is the spark at the beginning of all transformation, the courage in every leap, the whisper behind every calling.

We meet fellow travelers—some further along, some just beginning—all reflecting parts of ourselves. We engage with other "fools," mirrors of our own past naiveté or unrecognized potential. These encounters teach us about duality, co-creation, and perspective. Like light refracted through a prism, the Fool's journey becomes multifaceted—each experience illuminating a different angle of the self.

Conclusion: The Sacred Fool Within

The Fool is not a stage to be outgrown, but an archetype to be remembered, again and again. For every new beginning requires the heart of a Fool—open, curious, unburdened by the past, and ready to trust the unknown.

To embrace the Fool within is to say yes to life, yes to risk, yes to growth. It is to stand at the cliff's edge and know that, even if we fall, we are not falling apart—we are falling *into* ourselves.

In the end, The Fool's journey is our journey—cyclical, sacred, and soul-deep. The final destination is not a place, but a state of being: the realization that the journey *was* the destination all along.

"The Leap"

Upon the edge where reason ends,
A whisper stirs; the soul ascends.
No map, no path, no guiding star—
Just faith in who and what you are.

A satchel light with dreams untold,
A heart still young, a spirit bold.
The world below, the skies above—
You leap with trust, and not from shove.

The winds may roar, the night may fall,
Yet still you heed the silent call.
For in that step beyond the known,
You find a truth that's yours alone.

So, leap, dear one, the time is now,
No need to ask the where or how.
For every end begins anew—
And every Fool is born as You.

Journaling Prompts:

1. Where in my life am I called to take a leap of faith?

2. What fears or doubts hold me back from beginning anew?

3. What excites me about stepping into the unknown?

Guided Meditation:

Visualize yourself at the edge of a cliff under a bright sun. A white dog joyfully barks beside you. With deep breath, release fear and step forward — instead of falling, you float into radiant light. Whisper: *"The Universe carries me."*

Chapter 6
The Magician: Alchemist of Tarot

In the Tarot, **The Magician** is the first numbered card of the Major Arcana, yet it is numbered *1*, just after *The Fool (0)*—who represents pure potential. The Magician, in contrast, is the initiator—the one who takes raw potential and sets it into motion. He is the architect of manifestation, the master of focus, intention, and conscious creation. Where the Fool trusts the journey, the Magician steps into it with purpose.

He does not merely dream—he acts. With one hand pointed to the heavens and the other to the earth, he becomes the conduit between realms, embodying the Hermetic axiom: *"As above, so below."* He represents the bridge between the spiritual and the material, the invisible and the visible, the thought and its form.

Core Meanings of the Magician Card

1. Manifestation and Creative Power:

At his essence, The Magician embodies the ability to bring dreams into form. He symbolizes the power within us to *consciously* shape our reality. His presence in a reading is a reminder that we already have the tools we need—wisdom, inspiration, passion, emotion, and practicality—to create what we desire.

2. Willpower and Focused Intention:

The Magician teaches that focused thought, when channeled through aligned action, leads to transformation. He urges us not to wait for the world to shift but to *initiate* that shift through clarity, confidence, and conscious will.

3. Mastery of the Elements:

On his table lie the four suits of the Minor Arcana—wand, cup, sword, and pentacle—representing fire (spirit), water (emotion), air (mind), and earth (body). The Magician doesn't merely possess these tools; he *masters* them. They are extensions of his will, showing that true mastery involves integrating all aspects of self.

4. The Bridge Between Spirit and Matter:

His gesture—one hand raised to the sky, the other pointing to the ground—illustrates his role as an intermediary. He channels divine inspiration and grounds it into tangible reality. This is the act of sacred alchemy: transforming the invisible into the visible.

5. New Beginnings and Initiation:

The Magician often heralds the beginning of a journey, a fresh start, or the launching of a project that requires focus and inspiration. He invites us to step into our power and begin creating the life we envision.

6. Reversed Meaning:

When reversed, the Magician's energy becomes distorted. It may represent manipulation, illusion, scattered energy, or using one's power unethically. It reminds us that power, when misaligned, can be deceptive or misused.

Numerology and Astrology

The *Magician* tarot card is associated with the number 1 in numerology, symbolizing new beginnings, individuality, and the power of manifestation. Astrologically, it is linked to **Mercury** and the signs **Gemini** and **Virgo**, highlighting communication, intellect, adaptability, and precision. The card represents the ability to turn ideas into reality through focused intention, skill, and the harnessing of inner resources.

The Magician Archetype in Jungian Psychology

In Jungian thought, The Magician corresponds to the **Magus archetype**—the inner figure of wisdom, transformation, and spiritual insight. He is the one who sees beyond appearances, understands symbolic language, and perceives the interconnectedness of reality.

Key Aspects of the Magician Archetype:

- **Transformation Through Knowledge:**

The Magician seeks to transform both self and society through the power of understanding. This isn't knowledge for knowledge's sake—it is wisdom applied with intention.

- ### Intuition and Inner Vision:

He operates as much through intuition as through logic. He sees the patterns beneath events, the synchronicities, the hidden meanings. The Magician's strength lies in trusting inner sight as much as outer action.

- ### Ritual, Symbol, and Sacred Practice:

The Magician often engages with rituals, symbols, and sacred traditions—not out of superstition, but as a means of unlocking deeper truths. He recognizes that symbols are keys to the subconscious and that transformation begins within.

- ### Shadow of the Magician:

Like all archetypes, the Magician has a shadow. In distortion, he becomes the trickster, the manipulator, or the con artist—someone who misuses knowledge to deceive, control, or dominate. This warns of intellect without heart, power without wisdom.

Cultural and Mythological Echoes

Throughout mythology, literature, and modern life, the Magician archetype recurs:

- **Merlin** (Arthurian legend): the wise seer and guide.

- **Hermes / Thoth (Greek/Egyptian): gods of communication, magic, and divine knowledge.**

- **Alchemists and Mystics:** seekers who sought to turn base metal into gold—symbolically, to transform the human soul.

- **Scientists, Healers, Visionaries:** modern embodiments of the Magician who understand the laws of reality and work to shape them consciously.

In the everyday world, the Magician may appear as the innovator, therapist, teacher, or spiritual guide—those who wield insight with intention and use their understanding of systems to effect meaningful change.

Becoming the Magician: A Journey of Empowerment

To embody the Magician archetype is to reclaim your inner authority. It is to understand that you are not merely a passive observer in life, but a powerful creator. However, this power must be balanced with self-awareness, humility, and alignment with divine will.

Anyone can awaken their inner Magician:

- The young dreamer who dares to follow their calling.

- The seasoned soul who reinvents themselves after a fall.

- The seeker who rises from the ashes of past decisions and chooses to live consciously.

But without self-mastery, the ego often hijacks this power. The untrained ego seeks control from fear and separation. It grasps, manipulates, or overextends. The true Magician, however, is not interested in control over others—but in *sovereignty* over self.

True manifestation does not come from forcing the external world to bend to one's will. It arises from inner alignment. Reality is not something to be dominated—it is a mirror of the inner state. When our thoughts, feelings, and intentions are in harmony with our soul's truth, manifestation becomes effortless.

Final Reflection: The Alchemist Within

The Magician invites you to step into your creative authority. To see life as a canvas, your intention as the brush, and your belief as the color you paint with. He reminds you: **You are the spell, not the spellcaster. You are the magic, not the illusion.**

His ultimate message is one of sacred sovereignty:

To change your world, begin by mastering your inner one. To manifest a new reality, align with the divine spark within.

To become gold, remember—you were never base metal to begin with.

The true alchemist doesn't just transmute matter—he transforms **consciousness**. And the Magician, standing at the edge of the seen and unseen, beckons you forward. Not to believe in magic. But to *become it*.

The Magician Within

Within your hands, the tools reside,
Of earth, and flame, of air and tide.
With focused thought and heart aligned,
You shape the truth the stars designed.

One hand raised high to realms unknown,
The other roots you to your own.
You are the bridge of sky and land,
With silent power at your command.

A whisper sparks, a vision grows,
Through you, the stream of Spirit flows.
Not force, but flow—your truest might,
Is drawing shadows into light.

Yet heed the path, for power blind,
May tempt the ego, trap the mind.
But anchored deep in soul's intent,
All acts are pure, divinely meant.

So, speak the word, ignite the flame,
Transform the loss, release the shame.
You are the Magi, bold and true,
Creation lives and breathes through you.

Journaling Prompts:

1. What natural talents and resources do I already possess?

2. Where am I misusing or underusing my power?

3. How can I align my thoughts, words, and actions today?

Guided Meditation:

See yourself at a table with the four tools: wand, cup, sword, pentacle. A golden infinity glows above your head. You channel energy from the heavens into the earth. Affirm: *"As above, so below — I create with clarity."*

Chapter 7
The High Priestess Within:
Keeper of the Veil

In Tarot, **The High Priestess** is the guardian of inner truth, sacred mystery, and spiritual intuition. As the second card in the Major Arcana, she follows the Magician—not to act, but to *know*. Where the Magician looks outward to manifest, the High Priestess turns inward to listen. She is the stillness between breaths, the silence beneath sound, the threshold between the conscious and the unconscious.

Shrouded in robes of moonlight and seated before a thin veil that conceals the unknown, she invites you not to push forward, but to pause, reflect, and remember. She does not offer answers in words but in whispers—urging you to trust your inner guidance and honor the sacred mystery that life truly is.

Core Symbolism of the High Priestess

1. Intuition and Inner Knowing:

The High Priestess represents the deep well of inner wisdom we all possess. She calls us to trust our instincts, our gut feelings, and the quiet voice within that knows without proof.

2. Mystery and the Unseen:

She stands at the threshold of the hidden and the known. Her presence reminds us that not all truth is logical, and not all knowledge is meant to be revealed at once. Patience is part of the initiation.

3. Stillness and Receptivity:

Unlike the assertive energy of other archetypes, the High Priestess embodies sacred passivity. She teaches that clarity often arises in stillness, and that power sometimes lies in *not acting*—but in simply *being present*.

4. Feminine Energy and Spiritual Wisdom:

She embodies the Divine Feminine—intuitive, nurturing, mysterious, and receptive. She is aligned with the moon, tides, cycles, and the sacred knowledge held in silence.

5. Hidden Potential and Possibility:

Her presence suggests that talents, truths, and even destinies lie hidden beneath the surface, waiting to be discovered. But they require a descent into the self, beyond the ego, into the soul's depth.

Upright vs. Reversed Interpretations

Upright:

When appearing upright in a reading, the High Priestess advises trusting your intuition, stepping back from noise, and exploring your inner world. She invites reflection, dreams, study of esoteric knowledge, and spiritual listening.

Reversed:

Reversed, she may indicate blocked intuition, refusal to acknowledge inner truths, or avoidance of self-exploration. She may also signal secrets withheld, or guidance being ignored due to fear or external distraction.

Numerology & Astrology

The High Priestess tarot card is symbolically tied to the **number 2 in numerology** and the **Moon in astrology**, both of which emphasize themes of **intuition, duality, and the subconscious.**

- **Numerology (2):**

  Represents **balance and duality**, reflecting the High Priestess's role as a mediator between opposites (light/dark, masculine/feminine).

- Symbolizes **partnership and cooperation**, aligned with her empathetic and intuitive approach.

- Highlights **inner wisdom and intuition**, central to the High Priestess's spiritual nature.

- **Astrology (Moon):**

  The Moon governs **emotions, cycles, and the subconscious**, resonating with the High Priestess's depth and mystery.

- Encourages **emotional awareness** and **trust in intuition.**

- Associated with **divine feminine archetypes** (e.g., Artemis, Isis), reinforcing her connection to spiritual insight, independence, and sacred knowledge.

Overall, the High Priestess embodies **spiritual depth, sacred feminine energy, and intuitive understanding**, guided by the moon's cycles and the harmonious energy of the number 2.

In Jungian Psychology: The Inner Oracle

In Jungian psychology, the High Priestess archetype parallels the **Anima**—the feminine aspect of the soul that connects the conscious ego to the unconscious. She is the inner oracle, the mystic, the dreamer, and the guide who illuminates hidden aspects of the psyche.

1. The Subconscious Mind:

She represents the deep layers of the mind where buried memories, inherited beliefs, and hidden motivations reside. Through dreams, symbols, synchronicities, and inner prompts, she reveals the unseen forces shaping our lives.

2. The Divine Feminine Principle:

The High Priestess is the archetype of the sacred feminine—not in gender, but in energy. She is the receptive, intuitive, and spiritually attuned aspect of the psyche. She teaches that true wisdom often arises not from thinking, but from *listening* and *feeling*.

3. The Gateway to Inner Wisdom:

She is the keeper of the inner temple. To reach her, one must pass through the veil—symbolically stepping beyond superficial beliefs and external conditioning into the vast inner landscape of soul.

4. The Collective Unconscious:

Carl Jung spoke of the collective unconscious—a reservoir of inherited experiences and archetypes shared by all humanity. The High Priestess stands at the threshold of that realm, inviting us to retrieve the wisdom encoded in our spiritual DNA.

The Inner Journey and the Role of the High Priestess

As we journey through life, we are often conditioned to seek validation, meaning, and identity from the outside world. Our early years are shaped by the culture, family, and belief systems around us. These external influences become so ingrained that we rarely question them. We form identities based on survival, approval, or expectation.

Yet beneath these layers lies a deeper truth: **who we truly are**—not what the world has told us to be.

The High Priestess invites us to **remember**. To descend below the surface, where subconscious patterns and ancestral memories reside. Many of our instinctive reactions and emotional wounds are echoes of unprocessed trauma—some personal, others passed down through generations or absorbed from collective consciousness.

To truly awaken, we must uncover these imprints—not to judge them, but to *integrate* and *transmute* them.

She calls us to become conscious of:

- The unhealed wounds we've buried,
- The conditioned roles we've played,
- And the sacred power we've forgotten.

In this deep inner work, we meet not only our shadows but also our brilliance—our intuition, compassion, and the dormant abilities that were once veiled. We move from reactive living to *soulful* living.

Wisdom, Discernment, and the Path Forward

Life is rarely linear. The path to growth is not paved in certainty but marked with twists, illusions, and challenges. The High Priestess reminds us that we do not need to control every outcome. Instead, we are asked to *discern*—to trust the inner compass, especially when outer circumstances feel confusing.

She shows us that what appears as failure may be redirection. What seems like darkness may be a gestational void. That not all answers are meant to be immediate—and that silence, too, is sacred.

Even when we stumble, every misstep becomes a teacher. Through trial, stillness, and reflection, we realize that life does not merely happen *to* us—it happens *through* us, *for* us, and sometimes *because* of us.

Final Reflection: Beyond the Veil

The High Priestess is the keeper of the veil that separates the known from the unknown. But she does not guard it to keep us out—she guards it so that we might enter with reverence.

She calls you now, not to act, but to listen.

Not to fix, but to feel.

Not to seek outwardly, but to turn inwardly.

Within you lies a well of ancient knowing. Beneath your surface is a vast ocean of memory, truth, and divine intelligence. You are not separate from Source—you are an emanation of it.

And when you align with the voice within, you become not just a seeker of truth—but a **vessel of it**.

The Oracle Within

Beneath the noise, a whisper flows,
Where moonlight on the stillness glows.
She waits in silence, calm and deep,
Where sacred truths and secrets sleep.

She does not call with sound or flame,
But stirs you softly, speaks your name.
Not to command, or to explain,
But to dissolve your need for blame.

Her voice is felt, not always heard,
A knowing wrapped in thoughtless word.
She is the mirror, dark yet kind,
Reflecting what you've left behind.

So, close your eyes, release control,
Step past the gate, reclaim your soul.
The High Priestess, serene and wise,
Will guide you home through inner skies.

Journaling Prompts:

1. How do I currently hear my intuition speaking to me?

2. What secrets or mysteries am I resisting?

3. Where in my life do I need more stillness to listen deeply?

Guided Meditation:

Walk into a temple of moonlight. The High Priestess hands you a scroll. When you open it, you see a word or symbol only you can understand. Receive its meaning and affirm: *"I trust the wisdom within."*

Chapter 8
The Empress: Womb of Creation

The Empress tarot card, a central figure of the Major Arcana, radiates themes of nurturing, abundance, and creativity. She represents the feminine principle in its fullest expression, embodying motherhood, fertility, and the richness of the natural world. In readings, she often signals new beginnings—whether in the form of a child, a creative project, or the birth of a new venture. At her heart, the Empress reminds us of the importance of tending to our own needs and honoring the sacred act of self-care.

Key Meanings of the Empress

Nurturing and Caretaking

The Empress embodies maternal energy, encouraging us to nurture ourselves and others. This may involve caring for loved ones, supporting a creative project with dedication, or simply tending to one's own soul with compassion.

Abundance and Prosperity

Her presence herald's abundance in all forms—material wealth, emotional fulfillment, and spiritual joy. She invites us to embrace life's pleasures and recognize the overflowing gifts already surrounding us.

Creativity and Fertility

The Empress is strongly tied to fertility—both literal and symbolic. She represents the womb of creation, urging us to birth new ideas, bring dreams into form, and trust in our inherent creative power.

Connection with Nature

Rooted in the cycles of the Earth, the Empress calls us to ground ourselves in the natural world. She reminds us of the healing and harmony found in reconnecting with nature's rhythms.

Maternal Archetype

As the mother archetype, she symbolizes unconditional love, care, and the sustaining force of life. This archetype extends beyond individual mothers, encompassing the universal principle of creation and sustenance.

Reversed Meaning

In reversal, the Empress may indicate blocked creativity, neglect of self-care, or imbalance in relationships with a mother figure. It may also reveal scarcity consciousness or over-dependence on material security.

In a Reading, the Empress Suggests:

- A positive omen for family life or creative endeavors.

- A reminder to nurture oneself as lovingly as others.

- An invitation to embrace abundance and prosperity.

- A call to connect with one's creative essence.

- A gentle nudge toward self-love and holistic well-being.

Astrological and Numerological Associations

Planet Venus

The Empress is governed by Venus, planet of love, beauty, and harmony. She embodies Venus's sensuality and its power to attract abundance.

Zodiac Signs

- *Taurus*: Emphasizes comfort, sensuality, and material pleasures.

- *Libra*: Highlights balance, harmony, and relationship-centered abundance.

Number 3

The Empress is the third Major Arcana card. Numerologically, 3 represents creativity, expansion, and manifestation—the act of bringing spirit into form. It also signifies harmony, synthesis, and growth.

Jungian Psychology and the Mother Archetype

In Jungian terms, the Empress reflects the **mother archetype**—nurturing, protective, and life-giving. She symbolizes the unconscious wellspring of creativity and the instinct to foster growth.

Key Jungian Themes

- *The Mother Archetype*: Source of comfort, sustenance, and care.

- *Fertility and Abundance*: Symbolizing the flourishing of life in all forms.

- *Receptivity and Creativity*: Union of intuitive (feminine) and manifesting (masculine) forces.

- *Earthly Plane*: Connection to the personal unconscious and lived experience in the Fool's Journey.

- *Shadow Aspect*: When reversed, the archetype may manifest as neglect, overprotection, or material attachment.

The Empress thus marks a stage of individuation where the self-integrates nurturing and creative energies into a harmonious whole.

Concluding Reflection

Abundance is not a distant horizon to be chased, but a reality already present within and around us. The Empress teaches that gratitude is the key to unlocking life's fullness. When we choose to live in gratitude, we align with the natural flow of abundance, and the universe responds in kind.

Let us nurture ourselves, honor creation, and live in harmony with the cycles of nature. In doing so, we step into the sacred womb of abundance, where love, creativity, and growth flow without end.

Womb of Creation

In every seed, a world is born,
In gentle hands, the earth is sworn.
Through love's embrace, all life takes form,
The womb of creation, ever warm.

Gratitude opens the garden gate,
Abundance flows, both small and great.
In nature's song, her truth is known,
The Empress whispers: You are home.

Journaling Prompts:

1. What is seeking to be birthed through me?

2. How do I nurture myself as I nurture others?

3. What pleasures of life am I called to embrace?

Guided Meditation:

Sit in a lush meadow. The Empress crowns you with flowers. She places a seed in your hand. Plant it in the soil and watch it sprout instantly into what your soul most desires. Affirm: *"I create in harmony with abundance."*

Chapter 9
The Emperor:
The Sovereign Seat of the Self

The Emperor, the fourth card in the Major Arcana of the Tarot, stands as a powerful symbol of authority, structure, and dominion over one's reality. He represents the archetype of the ruler—the sovereign who governs not through brute force, but through wisdom, order, and conscious intent. Where The Fool begins the journey with trust and spontaneity, The Emperor represents the matured self who has built something enduring from that leap of faith.

He is the architect of civilization, the master builder who establishes foundations upon which others may stand. He governs the outer world, yet his greatest power comes from within—from knowing who he is and from embodying his divine right to rule.

Key Aspects of The Emperor

- **Authority and Control:**

The Emperor embodies rightful authority—not control for its own sake, but a grounded presence that commands respect. He knows his strength and uses it judiciously to lead, protect, and uphold justice.

- **Structure and Stability:**

He is the fortress in the storm. His presence represents the need for order, rules, and a clear framework—elements that create stability and reliability in life.

- ## Masculine Principle:

The Emperor archetype is aligned with the divine masculine energy—associated with logic, protection, provision, and decision-making. He balances the intuitive, fertile energy of The Empress with reason, planning, and execution.

- ## Leadership and Vision:

He leads with confidence and responsibility, not ego. He sets direction and inspires others to follow, knowing that his duty is service to a higher good.

- ## Discipline and Determination:

The Emperor's journey is one of dedication and perseverance. He reminds us that mastery is born not only from inspiration, but from sustained effort and inner resolve.

In Readings

- ## Upright:

Taking charge, asserting authority, creating structure, and establishing stability. It is a call to step into leadership in your life.

- ## Reversed:

Challenges with authority, resistance to control, overbearing behavior, or lack of inner discipline. A reminder to realign with authentic power.

- **In Love:**

The Emperor can signify a loyal, protective partner or a need for more clarity and boundaries in a relationship.

- **In Career:**

A sign of strong leadership, business acumen, and the power to manifest visions into reality through strategy and order.

Numerology and Astrology

The *Emperor* tarot card is linked to the number **4** in numerology, symbolizing stability, structure, and a solid foundation. Astrologically, it is connected to **Aries** and the planet **Mars**, highlighting themes of leadership, ambition, and assertive action. The Emperor embodies authority, order, and protective "fatherly" energy, encouraging the creation of a secure environment and the pursuit of goals with discipline and determination.

The Emperor in Jungian Psychology

In Jungian terms, The Emperor represents a crucial archetype on the path of individuation. He is the Father figure—provider of structure, law, and protection. His psychological role is to bring order to the chaos of the unconscious, to delineate boundaries, and to instill the values necessary for conscious life.

- **Positive Aspects:**

Leadership, discipline, responsibility, and the wise use of power to support growth—within oneself and others.

- **Negative Aspects (The Shadow):**

Rigidity, authoritarianism, emotional suppression, and an overemphasis on control. When disconnected from the heart or the soul, the Emperor becomes a tyrant.

- **Individuation and Integration:**

The journey of self-realization includes integrating the Emperor archetype—learning to lead oneself with inner strength and clarity. True sovereignty comes not from domination, but from aligned, conscious stewardship of the inner and outer realms.

The Master of Fate, the Captain of Soul

Perhaps the essence of The Emperor is captured best in the immortal words of William Ernest Henley:

"I am the master of my fate,

I am the captain of my soul."

These lines reflect the core of The Emperor's power: sovereignty. Not over others—but over oneself. The Emperor calls you to reclaim your throne, to stop living by default or in reaction, and to begin ruling your life with conscious intent and sacred responsibility.

Being "the master of fate" is not about controlling every outcome, but recognizing that your external world is the mirror of your internal kingdom. To master fate is to be intentional—to design a life that reflects your purpose, values, and divine potential. It means acting from alignment, not reaction.

To be "the captain of the soul" is to know that you are not the ego, not the roles, not even the thoughts that pass through the mind. You are the eternal being—the higher self—an expression of Divine Source. And until you reclaim this truth, you remain a wanderer without a compass.

The Emperor understands that *true authority* comes not from domination, but from alignment—with Self, with Soul, and with Source.

Becoming the Emperor of Your Own Life

The Emperor archetype invites us to embody a higher truth: that we are not merely subject to fate, but co-creators with it. His wisdom teaches us:

- That structure provides freedom.

- That discipline births clarity.

- That ruling the outer world begins with mastering the inner world.

Yet the Emperor's throne cannot be inherited. It must be earned—through trial, through pain, through the shedding of false identities. The soul must first descend into chaos, into disillusionment, into loss—only to rise again and reclaim its sovereignty.

This process is not one of accumulation, but of unveiling. Of removing the masks and stories that hide the truth. Power is not found in pretending to be more. Power is found in the naked essence of the soul—a blank slate of potentiality that needs no title to prove its worth.

Like the mythical King Arthur pulling Excalibur from the stone, the true Emperor is not chosen by force or birthright, but by inner purity, courage, and truth. Only when you recognize that you and the Divine are not separate, but one, can you wield such power with wisdom.

Conclusion: The Inner Throne Awaits

The Emperor stands as a mirror—asking: *Are you ready to rule your life?* Not with arrogance, not with fear, but with grace, clarity, and sovereignty?

To become the Emperor is to take full responsibility for your reality—not as punishment, but as liberation. It is to declare that your life is not random, but sacredly constructed, and that within you lies the wisdom, strength, and alignment to shape it.

This card is not merely about external leadership. It is about claiming your inner throne—the *sovereign seat of the Self*—and governing your life from soul, not shadow. For when the Emperor awakens within, the world no longer rules you. You rule your world.

The Sovereign Within

Upon the throne not forged by hand,
But shaped by truth, we learn to stand.
No crown is worn, no sword displayed,
Just soul reclaimed, no longer swayed.

From chaos born, in stillness grown,
The Emperor rises—not alone.
For in his heart, the Source resides—
And with that light, he gently guides.

Journaling Prompts:

1. Where do I need more structure in my life?

2. How do I relate to authority — both inner and outer?

3. How can I lead with wisdom instead of control?

Guided Meditation:

Stand before a throne of stone. The Emperor hands you a scepter and crown, reminding you of your inner authority. Feel grounded and steady. Affirm: *"I lead my life with strength and balance."*

Chapter 10
The Hierophant:
Keeper of Sacred Truths

THE HIEROPHANT

The Hierophant, also known as the Pope or High Priest in Tarot, stands as a powerful emblem of tradition, spiritual authority, and the structured wisdom passed down through generations. He is the guardian of sacred rites, the mediator between the divine and the human, and the channel through which spiritual truths are delivered in forms we can comprehend.

More than a religious figure, the Hierophant represents a bridge—a sacred transmission between worlds: the ethereal and the earthly, the eternal and the temporal. He reminds us that while spiritual truths may be timeless, their integration often requires form, ritual, and order.

Symbolism and Traditional Meaning

In classic tarot imagery, the Hierophant sits between two pillars, echoing the gateway of sacred knowledge. He wears a triple crown, symbolizing his dominion over the physical, mental, and spiritual realms. At his feet lie crossed keys—emblems of the power to unlock both the mysteries of heaven and the heart.

Upright Meaning: When upright, the Hierophant signals a time to seek guidance, align with tradition, or return to spiritual and communal roots. He invites us to trust in teachers, rituals, and institutions that offer wisdom and grounding. He also signals commitment—whether through marriage, vows, or shared spiritual paths.

Reversed Meaning: Reversed, this card invites introspection and rebellion. It challenges the status quo, asks us to question rigid belief systems, and empowers the individual to find their own truth outside of conventional frameworks. It's the soul's whisper to forge a new path guided by inner knowing.

The Hierophant in Love, Career, and Spirituality

In Love: This card often heralds traditional commitment—marriage, shared values, or unions built on long-standing beliefs. Reversed, it may call into question societal expectations around relationships, suggesting the need for unconventional or spiritually autonomous connections.

In Career: The Hierophant encourages mentorship, collaboration with institutions, and aligning one's work with values rooted in ethics and tradition. It's a card of structure, discipline, and respect for established hierarchies.

In Spirituality: Here, the Hierophant shines brightest. He is the sacred teacher, the spiritual guide, the transmitter of rituals and truths that offer grounding amidst the chaos of modern life. Whether through a guru, scripture, or sacred practice, he guides the seeker back to meaning and purpose.

Numerology and Astrology

The *Hierophant* tarot card is associated with the number 5 in numerology and the zodiac sign **Taurus**. The number 5 symbolizes change, learning through experience, and finding freedom within structure—mirroring the Hierophant's role as a spiritual teacher who bridges tradition and personal growth. Astrologically, Taurus adds themes of stability, values, and devotion to established beliefs. Together, these influences portray the Hierophant as a guide who helps others navigate their own path within the framework of established systems, blending innovation with tradition.

Jungian Archetype: The Hierophant as Spiritual Father

In **Jungian psychology**, the Hierophant embodies the **Wise Old Man** archetype—the Animus for women, or the collective representation of masculine logic, structure, and the pursuit of spiritual truth. He resides within the **collective unconscious**, surfacing when one seeks order, higher knowledge, or transition into a new phase of spiritual development.

Key Archetypal Attributes

Traditional Authority & Moral Compass: He represents the influence of culture, religion, and law on the individual psyche—calling us to honor the structures that preserve wisdom.

Initiation & Transformation: Much like a rite of passage, the Hierophant marks key transitions in life: spiritual awakenings, commitment ceremonies, or the acceptance of responsibility.

Voice of the Collective Unconscious: He is the societal echo of inherited norms, the quiet voice of the tribe, and the impulse to conform for collective survival and belonging.

Quantum Reflections: Structure in the Sea of Potential

From a quantum perspective, all existence begins as **pure energy—waveforms of unlimited potential**, undefined and boundless. As conscious beings, we collapse this potential into **form**—into particles, identities, experiences. To manifest in this physical world is to temporarily trade the infinite for the finite.

The **Hierophant**, then, symbolizes that very collapse: the embodiment of spiritual potential taking on **structure, hierarchy, and ritual** to be experienced and shared. The ego acts as a tether to this physical realm, navigating the illusion of separation and limitation for the sake of learning, expansion, and growth.

Through this entanglement with form—through roles like spouse, parent, student, citizen—we enter

agreements of structure. These societal constructs, often rooted in the Hierophant's domain, provide a stable stage for the soul's play. In this theater of form, we experience duality, contrast, and the full range of human emotion.

Yet even as we conform, our **higher self**—the wave—remains untouched, always whispering beneath the veil of forgetfulness. The Hierophant becomes both the veil and the key: the sacred paradox. He reminds us that the path to transcendence often passes through the very structures we once believed imprisoned us.

Contrast with the High Priestess: Exoteric vs. Esoteric Wisdom

While the **High Priestess** holds the mystery of the **inner world**, the Hierophant holds the scripture of the **outer world**. She whispers hidden truths through intuition and dreams; he chants sacred teachings in temples and institutions. One is mystical; the other theological. One conceals, the other reveals.

Yet together, they form the complete circuit of spiritual wisdom. The High Priestess is the moonlight, the Hierophant, the morning sun. One initiates us into mystery; the other instructs us in mastery.

The Sacred Sojourner's Journey

As sojourners in this realm of form, we walk a delicate line between **freedom and structure, individuality and conformity, formlessness and incarnation.** The Hierophant invites us to embrace the sacredness of this dance—not as restriction, but as a **soulful playground for consciousness to know itself.**

Through marriage and community, doctrine and ritual, we explore the layers of human experience. We agree, temporarily, to forget our divinity—to veil ourselves in rules, roles, and rituals—so that we may one day remember with awe who we truly are.

The Hierophant teaches us that even within limitation lies divine purpose. That **submission to sacred structure** is not weakness but wisdom—when chosen consciously. That belonging, tradition, and shared values are not chains, but bridges—doorways through which the soul can walk back home.

And finally, that once we have **gleaned all the wisdom** from form, from faith, from institutions and initiations— we are called to transcend them. To return not in rebellion, but in reverence, carrying the truth that:

The divine cannot be confined...

but sometimes, it wears robes and rings bells,

just to remind us where we left our light.

The Cloak of Sacred Form

Within the halls of stone and light,
Where candles burn through sacred night,
The voice of truth and inner sight,
Finds The Path Within

He speaks through rites, through law and creed,
A guide for souls in time of need.
His keys unlock the ancient way,
Where form and spirit softly pray.

Tradition holds a silent light,
A structure born from inner sight.
Though veiled in rules, the truth is near—
A sacred voice the heart can hear.

So, honor what the wise ones knew,
Yet seek the wisdom born in you.
For even in the old and worn,
The soul remembers why it's born.

Journaling Prompts:

1. What spiritual teachings most resonate with me?

2. Where do I follow tradition blindly rather than thoughtfully?

3. How do I serve as a guide or teacher to others?

Guided Meditation:

Step into a grand temple. The Hierophant blesses you, then invites you to kneel. He whispers a teaching meant only for you. Affirm: *"I receive wisdom and share it with integrity."*

Chapter 11
The Lovers: Divine Union

The Lovers tarot card, traditionally linked to relationships, love, and sacred choice, embodies far more than romantic connection. It speaks to the soul's yearning for union—within oneself, with another, and ultimately with the Divine. It marks a pivotal crossroads where the heart must lead, and discernment becomes paramount. This card calls not merely for decision, but for alignment—of values, desires, and truth.

Sacred Themes of The Lovers

1. Love and Soul Connection

At its most obvious level, *The Lovers* signifies relationships: the joy of romance, the sweetness of partnership, or the magnetic draw of kindred souls. This card highlights moments of connection that feel destined—when hearts speak the same language and intimacy is rooted in authenticity. Yet it also applies to profound friendships, soul contracts, and inner harmony.

2. The Crossroads: Choice and Consequence

Beneath its romantic layer, *The Lovers* is the card of choice. It often arises when we are faced with two diverging paths, each demanding reflection and clarity. The card invites us to weigh decisions not just with logic but through soul-guided wisdom. What aligns with your values? Which choice resonates with your truth? To love is to choose—intentionally, wholeheartedly, and sometimes, sacrificially.

3. Values, Integrity, and Inner Alignment

The card also prompts an inquiry into our personal values. What do you stand for? Are your actions in harmony with your beliefs? Whether in love, career, or spiritual calling, *The Lovers* demands integrity. It's not enough to follow the crowd or appease expectations; one must listen inward and walk the path of alignment, even when it's uncomfortable.

4. Harmony and Duality

The Lovers card reflects the dance of duality—masculine and feminine, light and shadow, spirit and matter. True harmony arises not by denying difference but by honoring and integrating polarity. Balance, not sameness, is the essence of sacred union.

Numerology & Astrology

The Lovers tarot card is closely tied to the **number 6 in numerology** and the **zodiac sign Gemini in astrology**, emphasizing **love, balance, communication, and conscious choice.**

- **Numerology (6):**
  - Symbolizes **love, harmony, and responsibility**, reflecting the card's focus on meaningful connections.

- Encourages **conscious decision-making,** particularly in relationships that impact personal growth and alignment with core values.

- **Astrology (Gemini):**

  Gemini, ruled by **Mercury,** emphasizes **communication, intellect, and adaptability**—key elements in building and maintaining relationships.

- Represents **duality and balance,** mirroring the Lovers' depiction of masculine and feminine energies and the need for mutual understanding in partnerships.

Overall, The Lovers card calls for **intentional choices, honest communication, and balanced relationships**, guided by both emotional resonance and intellectual clarity.

The Archetype of the Lover in Jungian Psychology

In Jungian terms, the Lover is an archetype of intimacy, creativity, and longing. This energy longs to merge, to feel deeply, to experience life in all its beauty and sensuality. It drives the pursuit of connection—emotional, physical, spiritual.

Light Attributes of the Lover:

- **Emotional Depth:** The Lover feels everything deeply, from joy to sorrow. This depth is their gift.

- **Creative Power:** Fueled by beauty and emotion, the Lover often births art, poetry, and transformative experiences.

- **Empathy and Compassion:** With an open heart, they can attune deeply to the needs of others.

- **Devotion:** The Lover gives fully—often to the point of sacrifice—for love and meaning.

Shadow Aspects of the Lover:

- **Codependency:** Without boundaries, the Lover may lose themselves in others.

- **Addiction and Escapism:** The pursuit of ecstasy or avoidance of pain may lead to unhealthy habits.

- **Possessiveness and Obsession:** Passion, when un-tempered by self-awareness, can become controlling or jealous.

- **Fear of Abandonment:** A deep-seated fear of loneliness may compel the Lover to cling or manipulate unconsciously.

Integration of this archetype means honoring the desire for connection without surrendering the Self. True intimacy arises when two whole beings meet, not when one seeks completion through another.

Divine Masculine and Divine Feminine: The Inner Union

The deeper meaning of *The Lovers* lies in the mystical union of the **Divine Masculine** and **Divine Feminine**—not as gender identities, but as archetypal energies that exist within all of us. This sacred polarity represents the dance of action and receptivity, reason and intuition, structure and flow.

The Divine Masculine is the energy of:

- Direction and purpose

- Strength, structure, and protection

- Leadership rooted in service

- Clarity, logic, and forward movement

- Action guided by integrity and wisdom

The Divine Feminine embodies:

- Intuition and inner knowing

- Compassion, nurturance, and softness

- Creative potential and emotional depth

- The mystery, receptivity, and spiritual insight

- The sacred womb of transformation and rebirth

When these forces are fragmented or imbalanced, life may feel disjointed—marked by indecision, chaos, or dominance. But when they unite—within oneself or in relationship—a new harmony emerges. The inner Lover awakens not just to passion, but to purpose. This sacred union births wholeness.

Manifestations of Divine Union

1. Within Oneself:

The first union begins inside. By recognizing and integrating both masculine and feminine aspects, we achieve inner balance. The intellect harmonizes with intuition. Action is tempered with presence. This inner marriage is the alchemy of wholeness.

2. In Relationships:

When two individuals come together having done their inner work, their union becomes a spiritual partnership. They don't complete each other—they complement, challenge, and elevate one another. This type of relationship fosters growth, mutual support, and sacred connection.

3. In Creation:

Balanced inner energies awaken creative genius. The masculine provides structure, the feminine offers flow. Together, they manifest visions into reality. Whether in art, business, or spiritual service, this is the birthplace of divine creation.

The Lovers as a Spiritual Invitation

The Lovers card ultimately asks: **Are you willing to choose love—not as a fleeting emotion, but as a path of awakening?**

Love, in this context, is not merely romance. It is union with your highest self. It is the choice to live with integrity, to align your decisions with your soul, and to walk the sacred path of wholeness.

To walk the path of the Lovers is to:

- **Choose with discernment** rather than impulse
- **Embrace both light and shadow** within and without
- **Open your heart** while honoring your boundaries
- **Balance freedom and connection**
- **Love consciously, fiercely, and wisely**

Closing Reflection

The Lovers is not merely about union with another—it is a mirror calling you home to your **inner beloved**, the Self-made whole through acceptance, integration, and love.

The meeting of two personalities is like the contact of two chemical substances: if there is any reaction, both are transformed." Carl Jung

Let this card remind you: divine union begins within. And from that sacred center, all other connections bloom.

"Sacred Union"

Within the heart, two voices speak,
One fierce with will, one soft and meek.
The mind may lead, the soul may yearn,
But love is found where both returns.

No war between the sun and moon,
They rise and set in sacred tune.
So too must we, both strong and kind,
Unite the halves and soul aligned.

In you, the lover waits to rise,
In mirrored gaze, see through disguise.
Not just in flesh, but flame and breath—
A dance of love that conquers death.

Mantra: For Inner Union

"I honor both the strength and softness within me.
I am whole. I am love. I am the union of light and shadow,
masculine and feminine, will and wisdom."

Journaling Prompts:

1. Where am I being called to make a soul-level choice?

2. What relationships reflect my highest self?

3. How do I honor both union and individuality?

Guided Meditation:

Stand between two paths. The Lovers appear, joined in light. They remind you that love is alignment with truth. You choose the path of the heart. Affirm: *"I choose love as my guide."*

Chapter 12

The Chariot: Victory Through Will

The Chariot, the seventh card in the Major Arcana of the Tarot, is a symbol of triumph, determination, and focused will. It marks a pivotal moment in the soul's journey—a moment when opposing forces must be harnessed and directed with clarity and intent. The Chariot is not merely about outward success or movement; it speaks to the inner mastery required to move forward with purpose through life's challenges.

Symbolism and Meaning

Upright, The Chariot speaks of:

- **Victory and Success:** You are aligned with your path, and through discipline and perseverance, triumph is within reach.

- **Willpower and Control:** You are being called to assert your authority over your circumstances, using your inner strength to guide your direction.

- **Self-Awareness and Focus:** Knowing yourself—your strengths, desires, and inner tensions—becomes the compass by which you navigate.

- **Action and Momentum:** This card signals forward movement. It's time to act, to progress, and to ride the current of momentum.

- **Direction and Guidance**: A clear vision and strong sense of purpose are your driving forces; you are no longer drifting but steering.

Reversed, however, The Chariot may indicate:

- **Lack of Direction or Control**: A sense of drifting, confusion, or inner conflict may cloud your path.

- **Obstacles and Delays**: External challenges or internal resistance may be slowing progress.

- **Loss of Focus or Motivation**: Disconnection from your deeper purpose may lead to misalignment or burnout.

- **Need for Reassessment**: It's a time to reflect—are your goals aligned with your soul's truth, or are you chasing illusions?

- **Inner Conflict**: Competing desires, or unresolved shadows may be at war within you, causing resistance and fragmentation.

Astrological and Archetypal Correspondences

The Chariot is astrologically aligned with **Cancer**, the sign of emotional intelligence, tenacity, and the power of the inner sanctuary. While Cancer is ruled by the

Moon, the card also shares themes with **Sagittarius**, which governs spiritual questing and the pursuit of higher knowledge. The blend of Cancer's intuitive nurturing and Sagittarius' directional fire reveals the Chariot's deeper message: balance the emotional realm with focused intent to reach your sacred destination.

The influence of the **Moon** deepens the card's ties to the subconscious and intuition, reminding us that true direction is not only set by logic but also by inner knowing. The horses or sphinxes pulling the Chariot often represent duality—light and dark, conscious and unconscious, masculine and feminine—underscoring the need to integrate and guide these opposing forces.

The Chariot in Jungian Psychology

In Jungian terms, The Chariot represents the **journey of individuation**—the sacred path of becoming a whole, integrated Self. The charioteer symbolizes the **ego** in its higher form: not as an adversary to the soul, but as a steward tasked with unifying the fragmented pieces of the psyche.

• **Individuation:** The process of integrating both the conscious and unconscious aspects of the self.

• **Willpower and Sovereignty:** The charioteer exerts conscious direction and discipline, using awareness to steer through life's chaos.

- **Balancing Opposites:** The Chariot urges us to reconcile inner dualities rather than be torn apart by them.

- **Shadow Confrontation:** The forward journey is not just outward—it is an inner reckoning. One must confront and embrace the shadow to move forward in truth.

- **Archetype of the Warrior and Hero:**

  It is the stage in the hero's journey where one takes up the mantle of conscious responsibility, wielding one's will in service of destiny.

Yet, pitfalls await obsession with control, rigid determination, or over-identification with success may cause imbalance. The spiritual warrior must remember that **victory without integration is hollow.** It is not enough to win battles; one must also bring home the wisdom of the war.

The Chariot as the Soul's Journey

At a deeper metaphysical level, The Chariot tells the story of the **soul's descent into duality.** In its purest form, the soul is whole, undivided, and radiant. But in this earthly realm, it chooses separation to learn, to evolve, and to expand. Governed by the constraints of polarity—light and dark, fear and love, scarcity and abundance—the soul enters a field where it must navigate the illusion of opposites.

Here, the **reptilian brain**—the primal survival instinct—often dominates, leading the self toward control, fear, and scarcity-based decisions. The Chariot represents the moment the soul begins to awaken from this unconscious mode of being. The charioteer seizes the reins, not to dominate life, but to **consciously direct it**. The goal is not conquest for conquest's sake, but **integration of all experiences**, both shadow and light, into a **harmonized whole**.

The path forward is not straight. It winds through conflict, desire, doubt, and determination. But with each challenge met through conscious will and inner clarity, the soul transforms.

This transformation is the **philosopher's stone**—the alchemical union of the fragmented self into gold. The Chariot is the vehicle of this alchemy, steering us not only through external conquests but toward **inner union**, toward the remembering of our divine essence.

Conclusion: Ride with Purpose

The Chariot invites you to **take the reins of your life**, not with brute force, but with deliberate consciousness. It urges you to **align with your inner truth**, confront your inner divisions, and navigate the outer world with strength, focus, and compassion.

Victory, then, is not found in domination, but in the **sacred synthesis** of all that you are. The journey of The Chariot is the journey home—to your essence, your wholeness, your divine will.

"He who conquers others is strong; he who conquers himself is mighty." Lao Tzu

Ride of the Soul

The chariot stands, the path is wide,
With light and shadow at each side.
Not to control, but to align—
The soul moves forward by design.

Through storms and silence, trials and grace,
The self finds truth in every place.
No crown to win, no need to roam—
The journey's end is coming home.

Journaling Prompts:

1. Where in my life do I need stronger direction?

2. How do I balance opposing forces within me?

3. What victory is calling me forward now?

Guided Meditation:

Ride in a chariot pulled by two sphinxes, black and white. With focused will, you direct them forward in unity. Affirm: *"I steer my life with clarity and purpose."*

Chapter 13

Strength: The Lion Within

The *Strength* card in tarot is not about domination or brute force. Instead, it speaks to a deeper, more enduring power—the kind born from within. It represents courage, patience, compassion, and the mastery of our instinctual nature through love rather than control. This card reminds us that authentic strength does not roar; it radiates, emanating from the calm confidence of a centered soul.

Core Meanings of Strength

- **Inner Strength and Courage**: This card highlights the power to endure life's trials through quiet resolve and inner fortitude. It's a reminder that the greatest victories often arise not from external conquest, but from self-mastery.

- **Emotional Mastery**: Strength invites us to tame volatile emotions and raw impulses with understanding, not repression. It's about learning to coexist with our "inner beast"—not by force, but by compassion.

- **Gentle Power**: The card teaches that influence wielded with kindness is more enduring than authority demanded through fear. Empathy and patience are true hallmarks of strength.

- **Self-Control and Patience:** It encourages conscious responses over reactive behavior, emphasizing mindfulness over impulsiveness.

- **Triumph Over Adversity:** This is the kind of strength that emerges when we persevere in the face of difficulty—not because it's easy, but because we are aligned with something deeper than fear.

Symbolism of the Card

- **The Woman:** She represents gentle influence, divine feminine energy, and the soft resilience of a nurturing heart. Her calm demeanor reminds us that power need not be loud.

- **The Lion:** Symbol of raw instinct, untamed desire, anger, or fear. Yet in her presence, the lion is subdued, not by violence but by reverence.

- **The Infinity Symbol:** Often above her head, it signifies the eternal, limitless capacity of the human spirit to grow, to love, and to evolve.

- **The Gentle Taming:** Rather than chains or force, the woman uses a soft touch, portraying an alchemical dance between will and instinct, higher self and ego.

Astrological and Numerological Correspondences

- **Zodiac Sign – Leo:** Associated with fiery passion, courage, leadership, and the heart. Strength, like Leo, is ruled by the Sun—symbolizing radiance, clarity, and vitality.

- **Number 8:** Often linked with the Strength card, this number represents balance, mastery, and achievement through sustained effort and karmic cycles.

Jungian Perspective: Strength as the Integration of the Self

In Jungian psychology, *Strength* is more than a symbolic figure—it becomes a mirror of the psyche in transformation. It reflects the journey of **individuation**: the lifelong process of integrating the conscious and unconscious aspects of the self.

- **Inner Resilience:** Jung believed true strength came not from suppressing emotions, but understanding them. Strength is the soul's ability to remain grounded in the storm, to feel deeply without being consumed.

- **Shadow Integration:** The lion represents the *shadow*—those instinctual or repressed parts of the psyche. The woman's gentle guidance reflects the invitation to meet our darkness with compassion, not judgment. Only when we acknowledge and embrace the shadow can we transform it.

- **Courage in Vulnerability:** Strength isn't about the absence of fear—it's about-facing fear with openness. It's about standing present in the unknown, unarmored but fully aware.

- **Anima/Animus Balance:** The card also speaks to the balance of masculine and feminine energies within all of us. The lion embodies the yang—assertive, instinctive, primal. The woman embodies the yin—receptive, calm, intuitive. Strength lies in their union.

The Sacred Dance of Duality

In our dualistic world, the soul is continually tested. Challenges arise not to break us, but to shape us. And in the midst of this sacred tension, *Strength* appears as a gentle guide.

Perhaps this card's image—a serene woman caressing the jaws of a mighty lion—captures a profound truth: that the real battle is not out there, but within. That the hero's journey is not one of slaying dragons, but of taming them. Of transforming rage into resolve. Fear into faith.

This archetype teaches us that aggression, often seen as a masculine force, must be channeled—not suppressed—by the calm, receptive, intuitive power of the divine feminine within each of us. It is she who softens the edges, who whispers wisdom into the roar of the beast.

In this light, *Strength* becomes the sacred fusion of opposites—the harmony of fire and water, will and surrender, instinct and grace. It reminds us that true power is not dominance, but direction. Not suppression, but integration.

A Radiant Force Within

As a card ruled by the **Sun**, Strength reveals the luminous potential within us. It is a solar archetype—not only because of its association with Leo—but because it burns away illusion, brings clarity, and fuels the life force that empowers our journey.

This strength is limitless. It does not deplete with use, but expands. It is the force that keeps us aligned when we are tempted to stray, the whisper of confidence when doubt creeps in, the warm center we return to again and again.

Final Reflections

The *Strength* card is a call inward. It urges us to recognize that our fiercest battles are often silent ones: learning to respond instead of react, to love when it's easier to fight, to remain soft in a world that tries to harden us.

In this card, we are reminded that vulnerability is not weakness—it is power refined through grace. That gentleness is not submission—it is courage matured. That to tame the lion is not to kill it, but to befriend it, so that instinct becomes wisdom, and power becomes love.

So when life roars, and the beast within stirs, may you find that quiet place of strength. May you respond not with force, but with presence. Not with fear, but with light.

And in doing so, may you realize:

The lion within you is not your enemy. It is your rawest truth—awaiting your love to become whole.

The Lion Within

Beneath the roar, a whisper speaks,
Not in might, but love it seeks.
A gentle hand, a fearless gaze,
Tames the fire, turns wrath to grace.

Strength is stillness, soft yet true,
The power to bend, yet still break through.
In heart's calm light, the wild is won—
The fiercest strength is harm to none.

Journaling Prompts:

1. Where do I confuse force with strength?

2. How can I tame fear with gentleness?

3. What does true courage mean to me today?

Guided Meditation:

Stand before a lion. Instead of fear, you touch it gently. The lion bows its head in peace. Affirm: *"My compassion is my true strength."*

Chapter 14
The Hermit: Light in the Silence

The Hermit stands alone, cloaked in silence, holding a lantern that glows not with external brilliance, but with the subtle light of inner truth. In the tarot, this archetype represents introspection, solitude, and the sacred journey inward. It signals a time to withdraw—not to escape the world, but to better understand it through the lens of our own soul.

This card does not speak loudly. It whispers. And in that whisper lies the call to turn away from the noise of life and enter a space of stillness where true wisdom resides. The Hermit does not seek answers outside—they have learned that the greatest guide is within. Through solitude, meditation, and quiet reflection, the soul reclaims its voice.

Themes of the Hermit

- **Introspection and Self-Reflection:**

  The Hermit invites us to turn inward, to gently explore the terrain of our inner world. It is a call to examine our thoughts, emotions, and beliefs without judgment.

- **Inner Wisdom and Trusting the Self:**

  This card reminds us that intuition is not a fleeting feeling—it is ancient, grounded wisdom. In solitude, the static clears, and the signal of our inner knowing grows stronger.

- **Spiritual Growth and Retreat:**

  The Hermit represents the seeker who retreats not out of fear, but to cultivate deeper truths. It marks a sacred pause, a spiritual sabbatical where healing and realignment occur.

- **The Quest for Truth:**

  The lantern the Hermit carries symbolizes the eternal search for truth—not the truth handed down by others, but the one buried beneath the layers of conditioning, ego, and illusion.

- **Guidance and Clarity in Stillness:**

  In a reading, The Hermit may point to the need for quiet contemplation before action. The answer you seek will not come through effort, but through presence.

Symbolic and Esoteric Insights

Astrologically, The Hermit aligns with **Virgo**, a sign associated with discernment, service, and purification. Ruled by **Mercury**, Virgo's analytical nature complements the Hermit's journey, emphasizing deep thought, inner dialogue, and personal refinement.

Numerologically, The Hermit is linked to the number 9—a number of completion, culmination, and endings. It marks the closing of a cycle, suggesting that before new beginnings arise, we must process what has been and distill its meaning.

The Hermit in Jungian Psychology

In Jungian terms, The Hermit represents the archetype of the wise guide or **"Wise Old Man"**—a figure who retreats from society to embark on a journey of individuation. It is a phase of necessary separation, where one integrates the conscious and unconscious, confronting shadows and outdated identities.

This archetype often surfaces during a **dark night of the soul**, when the psyche is undergoing deep transformation. What once gave us comfort now feels hollow. The roles we played lose their appeal. It is here, in this raw silence, that the soul begins its sacred unraveling.

A specific variation, the **Master-Turned-Hermit**, describes those who, after achieving worldly success or societal mastery, withdraw to tend to deeper inner work. Think of sages, monks, or artists who disappear from the public eye to preserve their truth.

The Hermit stage is not loneliness—it is sacred aloneness. It is the space where one strips away the masks worn for survival and meets the self that existed before the world had expectations.

Personal Reflection

There comes a point in every hero's journey when the path leads inward. The call to retreat becomes irresistible—not as escape, but as a return. We grow tired of external validation, of chasing meaning in noise. The soul yearns for authenticity.

In our solitude, we begin to hear again. First, the chaos. Then, the quiet. And finally—the truth. The Hermit teaches that enlightenment does not arrive in thunder— it dawns gently, like the morning mist lifting from a silent mountain.

This inward pilgrimage may at first feel like isolation, or even loss. But it is, in truth, the shedding of false selves. It is the healing of ancestral wounds. The realignment of our essence with Source. Here, in the quiet, we are not lost. We are finally found.

The Lantern Within

In quiet caves of thought and breath,
I wandered far from noise and death.
A lantern swung with golden grace
Illuminating my soul's true face.

I walked away from mirrored lies,
From veiled applause and hollow highs.
I met the silence, vast and deep,
And found the truths I could not keep.

No longer masked, no longer dim,
I heard the soul, a sacred hymn.
But I have found my inner truth.
The world may call it solitude.

Journaling Prompts:

1. Where in my life am I being called to retreat?

2. What wisdom have I gained through solitude?

3. What inner light am I ready to share with others?

Guided Meditation:

Climb a mountain at night. The Hermit greets you, raising his lantern. He lights your own lantern, showing you that the light was always within. Affirm: *"I follow my inner wisdom."*

Chapter 15
Turning the Wheel of Destiny

In the Tarot, the **Wheel of Fortune** is a powerful symbol of fate, cycles, and the ever-turning nature of life. It reminds us that change is inevitable—sometimes unexpected, often beyond our control—and that our growth lies not in resisting the spin of the wheel, but in learning to respond with awareness, grace, and trust.

This card suggests that you may be entering a new phase—perhaps a fortunate rise or an uncomfortable fall—and your experience of it will depend not on circumstance alone, but on your consciousness and your choices.

Upright Meaning

- **Change and Cycles:** Life is not linear, but circular. The Wheel of Fortune echoes the seasons, tides, and celestial rotations—everything rises, falls, and rises again.

- **Destiny and Fate:** Events may be unfolding in alignment with a larger cosmic plan. Synchronicities may appear, nudging you toward your soul's contract.

- **New Opportunities:** This card can herald unexpected blessings or shifts that open doors—if you're present enough to walk through them.

- **Good Fortune and Luck**: Often a symbol of prosperity or favorable timing, it asks you to stay open to the unseen support guiding your journey.

- **Surrender and Flow**: Resistance is futile when the wheel turns. Embrace the flow rather than clinging to what was.

- **Karma and Consequence**: What you've planted may now be coming to harvest. The card honors the law of cause and effect.

Reversed Meaning

- **Delays and Frustration**: You may feel stuck in a holding pattern or face setbacks. Trust that the wheel is still turning, even if you can't yet see movement.

- **Resistance to Change**: Clinging to control or fear of the unknown may be blocking your growth.

- **Victim Mentality**: You may be blaming fate rather than owning your role.

- **Missed Opportunities**: Indecision or fear may cause you to overlook a pivotal moment of change.

Symbolism and Imagery

- **The Wheel**: At the center is the ever-spinning wheel of life—reminding us of the constancy of change.

- **Mythic Figures**: The sphinx, serpent, and Anubis or similar archetypes represent the rise, fall, and transformation within all cycles.

- **The Four Creatures**: The lion, ox, eagle, and man—symbols of the fixed zodiac signs—stand in the corners, reminding us that amidst change, some truths remain constant.

Astrological and Numerological Significance

- **Jupiter's Influence**: The Wheel of Fortune is ruled by **Jupiter**, planet of expansion, abundance, and growth. Its energy brings possibility, opportunity, and divine timing.

- **Number 10 → 1**: The number 10 symbolizes completion, but also new beginnings. Reduced to **1**, it speaks of leadership, initiation, and the birth of something new.

- **Fixed Signs**: The presence of **Taurus, Leo, Scorpio, and Aquarius** reinforces the message that while the wheel spins, the core of your soul remains anchored in eternal truths.

Psychological and Archetypal Depth (Jungian Perspective)

In **Jungian psychology**, the Wheel of Fortune—sometimes called *Rota Fortunae*—represents the unconscious patterns that shape our lives. It reflects the rhythms of the psyche, where we repeat cycles until we bring them into awareness and transform them.

- **Cyclic Patterns:** Just as nature moves through seasons, our inner world repeats emotional and psychological patterns until we learn their lessons.

- **Fate and Free Will:** Jung taught that by becoming conscious of the unconscious, we reclaim agency in shaping our lives. The wheel turns, but we learn how to ride it with grace.

- **Individuation:** The card marks a pivotal point in the hero's journey—the moment of realization that fate is not imposed, but discovered, aligned with, and ultimately shaped by our own evolving consciousness.

In Love and Relationship Readings

- **Fated Encounters:** This card may signify a soul contract being activated—a destined meeting or pivotal shift in a relationship.

- **Turning Points:** The wheel can usher in changes—deepening a bond, ending a cycle, or beginning anew.

- **Growth through Cycles:** Relationships move through phases; what is tested may also be transformed.

A Reflection on Destiny

Destiny, in its truest form, is not a fixed point written in the stars. It is the unfolding of our highest truth in alignment with divine timing. It is a living, breathing dance between choice and surrender, will and grace. We are not simply at the mercy of fate—we are co-creators, tuning our lives through thought, emotion, intention, and vibration.

Like music, our lives vibrate in resonance with the inner frequencies we emit. The more conscious we become—of our beliefs, of our energy—the more deliberate we become in shaping the reality we experience. Each thought is a ripple. Each emotion, a chord. Each choice, a turning of the wheel.

The Wheel of Fortune reminds us that we are not here merely to endure what is fated—but to awaken, remember, and rise into what is possible. We are not passengers on a journey dictated by stars, but pilots of perception, navigating the soul's spiral home.

Closing Thought

When the wheel turns, don't ask "Why me?"—ask, "What now?"

Let every twist be an invitation to rise. Let every fall be a lesson in surrender. And let every return to the top remind you that nothing is lost, only transformed.

In every spin of the wheel, the soul has a chance to realign—with truth, with love, and with its infinite potential.

Whispers of the Wheel

The wheel it turns, with silent grace,
Through shadowed fall and sunlit place.
No hand can stop its destined spin,
But hearts awake can shape within.

A crest may lift, a trough may fall,
Yet soul remains through rise and stall.
It's not the change that shapes the soul,
But how we dance when tides unroll.

We are not leaves adrift in storm,
But sparks of light in human form.
When we align with truth and trust,
The wheel obeys—because it must.

So let it turn, and let it teach,
For every fall brings wisdom's reach.
Each cycle births a sacred key,
Unlocking who we're meant to be.

Let go the grip, release control,
The wheel turns not to take, but soul.
And in the silence, soft and deep,
Your destiny begins to speak.

Journaling Prompts:

1. What cycles are repeating in my life?

2. How do I react to change — with fear or faith?

3. How can I align myself with the flow of life?

Guided Meditation:

See a great wheel turning before you. Step onto it. Instead of spinning chaotically, it lifts you upward with grace. Affirm: *"I trust the cycles of destiny."*

Chapter 16
Justice: In Alignment with Truth

The **Justice** card in the Tarot stands as a powerful symbol of truth, fairness, and the balancing of scales—both within and without. It calls for ethical introspection, responsible action, and decisions rooted in integrity. More than just a card about legal matters, Justice invites us to examine how we align with universal principles of order and morality.

Key Themes of the Justice Card

- **Fairness and Balance**

    Justice is not limited to courtroom law; it speaks to cosmic balance—the equilibrium that governs our choices and their consequences. It reminds us that our internal world must be just if we are to create harmony in our external life.

- **Truth and Accountability**

This card compels us to stand in truth, acknowledge our actions, and accept their outcomes. It emphasizes that true empowerment arises not from control, but from taking full responsibility for our reality.

- **Wise Decision-Making**

Justice calls for discernment. It urges us to weigh both sides of any matter—logic and emotion, self and other, rights and responsibilities—before reaching a resolution.

- **Legal and Moral Implications**

In readings, Justice may indicate involvement in legal matters, contracts, or formal decisions. But symbolically, it reflects the deeper laws of karma and moral accountability.

- **Reversed Justice**

When reversed, the card warns of imbalance, dishonesty, or unresolved injustices. It may prompt reevaluation, encouraging course correction before imbalance breeds disillusion.

Astrological, Numerological and Mythological Correspondences

The Justice card is intimately connected to **Libra**, the zodiac sign ruled by **Venus**, and philosophically grounded in the karmic lessons of **Saturn**.

- **Libra** brings the motif of the scales—symbolizing the need for harmony, objectivity, and relational fairness.

- **Venus** imparts a sense of beauty and equilibrium in relationships, reminding us that justice is not merely cerebral but also compassionate.

- **Saturn**, the taskmaster, adds weight, responsibility, and the inescapability of consequences to the Justice archetype.

The **Justice** card in Tarot is associated with the number 11, a **master number** in numerology, which can also be reduced to 2. Both numbers emphasize themes of **fairness, balance, and conscious decision-making.**

- **Master Number 11:**

- Represents **heightened intuition, insight, and spiritual awareness.**

- Often linked to **growth through challenge**, encouraging truth, clarity, and ethical integrity.

- **Reduced Number 2:**

- Symbolizes **duality, partnership, and balance**, reinforcing the need to weigh all sides carefully.

- Aligns with **diplomacy and justice**, encouraging thoughtful and unbiased decision-making.

Overall, the Justice card blends the **spiritual discernment of 11** with the **harmonizing logic of 2**, urging fair judgment and accountability rooted in both intuition and reason.

From a mythological lens, **Themis**, the Greek goddess of divine law and order, reinforces the sacredness of Justice. She represents more than legal authority—she is the voice of natural order and spiritual rectitude.

Jungian Psychology and the Justice Archetype

In **Jungian psychology**, Justice is more than an external virtue; it is an inner archetype tied to the process of **individuation**—the journey toward wholeness.

- **The Justice Archetype** symbolizes our innate drive for fairness, order, and ethical living.

- **The Shadow Side of Justice** can manifest as rigid judgment, moral superiority, or projection of blame—obstacles that hinder self-integration.

- **Inner and Outer Balance** must be cultivated, for without inner harmony, any external attempts at justice remain performative or short-lived.

- The role of the **Self** in Jungian thought guides us to integrate opposing forces within—ego and shadow, rationality and emotion—so we may live in right relation to ourselves and others.

- **Justice in Dreams** often surfaces as symbols (e.g., courts, judges, scales) representing unresolved inner conflicts or ethical dilemmas asking to be addressed.

Through the lens of individuation, we see that Justice is not a destination but a dynamic equilibrium we must constantly cultivate in both personal and collective realms.

Mystical Perspectives: Duality and Detachment

In the soul's journey, **duality** is an essential classroom. We experience joy and sorrow, victory and failure, light and shadow—not to remain trapped in these polarities, but to transcend attachment and recognize the deeper unity beneath them.

If we cling too tightly to any one pole—be it pleasure or pain—we risk becoming paralyzed by form and losing touch with the soul's higher calling: **experience, awareness, and expansion.** Justice, then, is not a fixed verdict but a flowing rhythm in the dance of life, where balance is moment-to-moment attunement.

Ancient Wisdom: Justice in Mithraism

The ancient mystery religion of **Mithraism** offers a profound archetype in the god **Mithras**, who embodies truth, cosmic order, and the upholding of sacred contracts.

- **Mithras** as guardian of justice ensures the sanctity of oaths and the righteousness of actions. His solar connection symbolizes enlightenment and the triumph of divine law over chaos.

- The **Mithraic initiations**, progressing through seven grades, reflect a symbolic path toward moral purification and alignment with cosmic justice.

- Belief in **justice beyond death**, with celestial rewards or infernal consequences, parallels the idea of karmic balance across lifetimes—a central tenet in many mystical traditions.

Concluding Reflection: Justice as the Soul's Compass

Justice is not merely about retribution or external fairness. It is the **inner compass of the soul**, constantly pointing toward alignment with truth, integrity, and wholeness.

To walk the path of awakening, we must learn to **balance**—not just scales of logic and emotion, but the deeper polarities of being. We must accept both light and shadow, face the consequences of our actions, and remain unattached to outcome while devoted to right action.

Justice calls us to be clear mirrors for our own soul: to seek truth over comfort, accountability over avoidance, and balance over chaos. It is the voice within that whispers, *"Act with integrity, and let the universe take care of the rest."*

And in this unfolding, we come into alignment not only with cosmic law but with the divine nature within us— ever just, ever whole.

"Scales of the Soul"

Justice stands with steady grace,
A mirror held to time and space.
She asks not vengeance, nor loud decree,
But truth within, to set us free.

Balance born from honest sight,
Choosing wrong or choosing right.
In silence deep, the soul will see,
That justice starts with you and me.

Journaling Prompts:

1. Where am I being asked to take responsibility?

2. What truth do I need to face honestly?

3. How can I restore balance in my relationships?

Guided Meditation:

Stand before the scales of Justice. Place a burden on one side. The sword of clarity strikes, balancing the scales. Affirm: *"I live in truth and integrity."*

Chapter 17

The Hanged Man:
When Surrender Becomes Power

The *Hanged Man* tarot card invites us into a space of deep paradox—where stillness leads to movement, surrender begets strength, and letting go becomes the catalyst for transformation. As the 12th card of the Major Arcana, the Hanged Man signifies a pivotal turning point, urging us to release control and embrace a different way of seeing and being.

Core Themes of the Hanged Man

- **Sacrifice and Surrender:** At its essence, the Hanged Man reflects the power of voluntary sacrifice. It speaks to the wisdom in choosing to pause, release outdated habits or attachments, and yield to a greater purpose—even when it involves temporary discomfort or loss.

- **New Perspectives:** His inverted posture is symbolic of seeing the world from a new vantage point. It's an invitation to shift awareness, question assumptions, and awaken to higher insight.

- **Waiting and Suspension:** The Hanged Man often emerges during times when forward momentum seems stalled. These periods of liminality are not punishments but initiations—sacred pauses in which we are asked to reflect, recalibrate, and receive wisdom that only stillness can offer.

- **Spiritual Transformation:** Just as the caterpillar must dissolve into formlessness before becoming the butterfly, the Hanged Man guides us through a symbolic death of the ego or old identity, clearing the way for rebirth and evolution.

Upright and Reversed Interpretations

Upright, the Hanged Man calls for:

- **Patience and Trust** in life's unfolding

- **Embracing the Unknown** with faith rather than fear

- **Releasing Control** to find deeper inner peace

- **Gaining Insight** through altered perception or contemplation

Reversed, it can signal:

- **Resistance to Change** or inner stagnation

- **Fear of Letting Go** and clinging to outdated beliefs

- **Worthless Sacrifice,** where energy is misdirected or drained

- **Emotional Paralysis**, a refusal to shift perspective despite mounting pressure

In Daily Life: Love and Career

In **relationships**, the Hanged Man suggests stepping back to gain perspective. It may highlight the need for surrendering expectations, allowing love to unfold naturally, or pausing to reassess compatibility. For singles, it's a reminder that forced connections rarely yield joy. For couples, it may call for deeper understanding or necessary sacrifices to elevate the relationship.

In **career**, this card may signify a liminal phase—one of transition, uncertainty, or quiet reevaluation. It asks us to reflect on whether we're chasing external success at the expense of inner alignment and encourages creative approaches born from non-linear thinking.

Astrology, Numerology, Symbolism and Esoteric Correspondences

The Hanged Man is astrologically linked to **Neptune** and the **12th House**—realms of mystery, dreams, dissolution, and surrender. In the Hebrew alphabet, it corresponds to **Mem**, the "waters," signifying immersion into the subconscious. The image of the man hanging from a T-shaped cross (the tau cross of **Saturn**) roots the experience in material reality, even as the mind transcends into otherworldly realms.

The **Hanged Man** tarot card is linked to the number **12**, which reduces to **3** in numerology. This numerical progression reflects the card's deeper message of **transformation through surrender.**

- **Number 12:**

    Signifies the **end of a cycle** and the **threshold of new understanding or growth.**

- Implies a **pause for reflection** before moving forward.

- **Reduced Number 3:**

- Represents **creativity, self-expression, and new beginnings.**

- Suggests that clarity and renewal often arise from stillness or inner contemplation.

- **Core Message:**

- Though the Hanged Man implies **sacrifice and suspension,** its essence is about **shifting perspective, letting go,** and gaining insight through non-resistance.

- Through surrender, one unlocks **creative breakthroughs and inner growth**

The spiritual symbolism is profound: by suspending ourselves—our judgments, identities, expectations—we gain access to the **"watery mind-stuff"** beneath surface reality. We pierce the illusions of separateness that the senses reinforce and touch the underlying unity of all things.

Ultimately, the Hanged Man teaches that **true freedom and transformation arise when we release control and allow space for a new vision to emerge.**

Jungian Depth Psychology Perspective

In Jungian terms, the Hanged Man represents an **initiation into the unconscious.** The suspension reflects a descent—a necessary turning inward to confront shadow elements and reconfigure the psyche.

- **Surrender** becomes not passive resignation, but active participation in transformation.

- **Perspective shift** mirrors individuation: the death of ego-driven consciousness and the birth of a more integrated Self.

- **Reversal of values** allows us to reorient from the external world to inner truth.

The myth of **Odin**—who hung himself from the World Tree, Yggdrasil, to gain wisdom—echoes this archetype. Insight, in this view, is won not through conquest, but through surrender and self-sacrifice.

The Paradox of Surrender

Surrender, in this deeper context, is counterintuitive. Conditioned by primal instincts to fight or flee, we equate surrender with weakness or defeat. It's only when these strategies fail—when striving leads to burnout or resistance amplifies suffering—that we entertain the radical notion of letting go.

Yet there is a **second surrender**—not to a known adversary, but to the **great unknown**. This surrender is not giving up, but giving over: a conscious trust in forces larger than the rational mind can grasp. It's a spiritual posture of openness, patience, and alignment.

We often seek to master life by controlling outcomes. But control is a mirage. The more we chase certainty, the more chaos evades our grasp. It is in **stillness**, **yielding**, and **non-doing** that true mastery is found.

Concluding Reflection: Becoming the Hanged One

To embody the Hanged Man is to become the bridge between the visible and invisible, the external and internal, the known and the mysterious. It is to courageously **hang in suspension**, not as a victim, but as a seeker of truth. It is to realize that power does not only lie in action, but in **presence**—in the sacred pause before the leap, the breath before the rebirth.

The Hanged Man teaches us that surrender is not the end of power, but its **transmutation**. Only through letting go can we be lifted. Only in dying to what was can we become what we are meant to be.

"Sometimes we must go upside down to see right side up. In stillness, we awaken. In surrender, we rise."

In Stillness, I Rise

I hung between the earth and sky,
Not to fall, but learn to fly.
Through letting go, I came to see,
The chains were never outside me.

No need to fight, no need to run,
The battle ends when we become one.
In silence deep, the truth appears—
What we resist is what we fear.

So, upside down, I found my grace,
Not in the race, but in the space.
In yielding to the great unknown,
I touched a strength I'd never known.

Journaling Prompts:

1. What situation am I resisting that requires surrender?

2. How can I see my current challenge from a new angle?

3. What wisdom emerges when I let go of control?

Guided Meditation:

Visualize yourself hanging upside down on a tree, but at peace. A radiant halo surrounds your head. From this new angle, clarity dawns. Affirm: *"I release control and trust divine timing."*

Chapter 18
Death: Portal to Transformation

In Tarot, the **Death card (XIII)** is often misunderstood, conjuring fear and apprehension. Yet in truth, it rarely signals literal death. Instead, it represents **transformation, transition, and the sacred art of letting go.** It marks the end of a chapter, a necessary clearing of the old to make way for the new. Death in Tarot is not a full stop—it's a turning point.

Core Meanings of the Death Card

- **Endings and Beginnings**

  Death symbolizes the close of a significant life phase or identity. Whether it's a relationship, a belief system, or a role we've outgrown, this card brings the message: it's time to release what no longer serves your highest self.

- **Transformation and Rebirth**

  Much like the metamorphosis of a caterpillar into a butterfly, Death points to deep transformation. It speaks to a spiritual rebirth—shedding old skins to reveal a more aligned, authentic self.

- **Letting Go**

  Death asks us to surrender to life's natural cycles. Rather than resisting change, we are invited to trust the process of renewal. It's in letting go that we make room for the unknown magic that seeks to enter.

Astrological and Numerological Reflections

In **astrology**, death and transformation are associated with the **8th house, Scorpio**, and the planet **Pluto**—all of which govern the mysteries of death, rebirth, sexuality, and the occult.

- **Scorpio & Pluto:** Signify intensity, deep transformation, and the destruction of illusions.

- **8th House:** Rules over shared resources, transformation, and existential mysteries.

In **Vedic astrology**, the **maraka planets** and planetary periods (dashas) relate to endings, while the 3rd and 8th houses are examined to understand the soul's karmic cycles and longevity. However, both Western and Eastern systems emphasize that astrology is not a tool for predicting physical death—it is a map for understanding life's transitions.

In **numerology**, while **Life Path Numbers** reveal karmic lessons and key phases of life, they are not used to predict physical death. Instead, they illuminate **themes of evolution**, helping us understand the spiritual challenges we are here to face and overcome

Jungian Psychology: Death as a Symbol of Individuation

From the lens of **Jungian psychology**, death is not solely about physical demise. It is a **symbolic archetype** representing psychological death—**the dissolution of the false self** so that the true self may emerge.

- **Psychic Death and Rebirth**

  Jung described "psychic death" as the surrender of outdated identities, beliefs, and ego structures. This death opens the door for **individuation**, the process of becoming whole and fully integrated.

- **The Death Archetype**

  Death, as an archetype, is both feared and revered. It is the gateway between what was and what will be. To confront it consciously is to invite growth, maturity, and deeper self-knowledge.

- **The Second Half of Life**

  Jung emphasized that aging naturally brings us closer to the reality of death. This phase urges us to turn inward, seek meaning beyond material pursuits, and prepare for spiritual transcendence.

- **Dreams and Inner Guidance**

  Dreams of death may signify the end of a cycle or the beginning of transformation. Encounters with deceased loved ones in dreams may reveal subconscious healing or communion with the archetypal realm.

Mystical Wisdom: Death as Initiation

Many spiritual traditions treat death as an **initiation**—a sacred transition rather than an end.

In **Mithraism**, for example, death was honored through ritual. The god **Mithras** upheld truth, justice, and cosmic order. As a solar deity, Mithras symbolized the **light that follows darkness**, affirming that death leads to rebirth and the triumph of divine truth.

- **Initiation and Moral Purification**

  The Mithraic mysteries viewed death as part of a soul's journey toward moral refinement and union with the divine.

- **Light of the Sun**

  Mithras's solar connection reinforces the symbolism that through the darkness of death comes the clarity of spiritual light.

Concluding Reflection: The Sacred Return

To the ego, death is terrifying—an erasure of identity, control, and form. But to the **soul**, death is a return: a **homecoming to truth**, a sacred passage back into oneness. Life, death, and rebirth form an eternal spiral— **the breath of existence itself.**

From this higher lens, we see that death is not something to fear, but to revere. It teaches us the art of impermanence, the power of surrender, and the freedom of release. We honor those who have crossed over not by clinging, but by continuing their light within us.

The Death card reminds us that nothing truly ends— everything transforms. The body may return to dust, but love, consciousness, and memory are eternal threads in the tapestry of existence.

Let us then meet death, not with dread, but with **trust in the unfolding**, knowing it is through death that the soul is reborn.

Veil of Change

A breath, a pause, a closing door,
Yet something waits we've known before.
Not end, but shift—new skies to roam,
The soul departs, returning home.

What falls away was never lost—
It shaped the path our spirit crossed.
Through death, we rise—reborn, set free,
Becoming who we're meant to be.

Journaling Prompts:

1. What is ending in my life that I must honor?

2. What am I afraid to release?

3. What new beginning awaits me beyond this ending?

Guided Meditation:

Walk through a forest of falling leaves. Death rides past, silent but kind. You lay down what no longer serves you. A butterfly emerges before you. Affirm: *"I embrace endings as gateways to rebirth."*

Chapter 19
Temperance: The Still Point of Becoming

The Temperance card in Tarot represents the sacred art of balance, moderation, and patience. It calls us to live not in extremes, but in harmony, blending the parts of our lives into a meaningful whole. When Temperance appears in a reading, it often signals a time for measured action, integration, and mindful equilibrium.

Key Interpretations:

- **Balance and Harmony**

  Temperance teaches the importance of balance in all areas of life—between work and rest, giving and receiving, effort and surrender. It is the invitation to live with grace and intentionality.

- **Moderation**

  The card gently warns against indulgence or rigidity. It encourages the middle path—an approach that fosters sustainability, growth, and inner peace.

- **Patience and Timing**

  Temperance reminds us that true transformation unfolds in its own time. Rushing the process leads to imbalance. Trusting divine timing allows things to fall into place naturally.

- **Self-Control**

  It asks us to temper our emotions, impulses, and reactions, cultivating wisdom and clarity rather than reactivity.

- **Integration**

  Above all, Temperance calls for integration—blending opposites into something new, greater, and more complete. Whether it's reconciling inner conflicts or finding unity in relationships, Temperance is the alchemy of the soul.

Upright and Reversed Meanings

- **Upright:**

  A sign of inner peace, calm resolution, and successful integration. You're learning to navigate life's challenges with poise and patience.

- **Reversed:**

  Points to imbalance, overindulgence, or emotional discord. It may be time to re-center, release compulsions, or reflect on your energetic alignment.

Symbolism of the Card

The angel depicted in the Temperance card has one foot on land and one in water—signifying balance between the material and spiritual realms. Pouring water between two cups, the angel blends opposites in an eternal flow, showing that wholeness is not static but dynamic and evolving. A path in the distance, leading to a radiant sun, suggests that this process of integration leads to enlightenment and a brighter future.

Astrological & Numerological Insights

- **Sagittarius & Jupiter:**

    Temperance is astrologically tied to **Sagittarius**, the seeker of truth, and ruled by **Jupiter**, the planet of expansion and wisdom. This pairing supports exploration, philosophical growth, and the integration of multiple viewpoints.

- **Number 14 → 5:**

    Temperance is card **XIV (14)** in the Major Arcana. In numerology, 14 reduces to **5**, which signifies **change, adaptability, and transformation**. While Temperance may appear serene, it is deeply transformative—asking us to flow with change rather than resist it.

Jungian Psychology Perspective

In the lens of Jungian psychology, Temperance represents the **integration of opposites** within the psyche—light and shadow, masculine and feminine, conscious and unconscious. This alchemical union leads to **individuation**, the journey toward becoming a whole, self-aware individual.

Temperance is not simply restraint—it is *dynamic harmony*. It teaches us that wholeness is born not by eliminating our contradictions but by embracing and balancing them.

- **Integration of Opposites:**

  Embracing all parts of ourselves is the foundation for psychological and spiritual maturity.

- **Middle Way:**

  Avoiding extremes helps foster stability, empathy, and wisdom.

- **Healing through Wholeness:**

  This inner reconciliation is a powerful force for healing and authentic self-expression.

Vibration, Resonance, and Sacred Harmony

In the grand symphony of existence, everything vibrates. Life itself is a dance of frequencies—thoughts, emotions, intentions—all playing a role in the energy we emit and receive.

Temperance, in this context, is the art of **energetic attunement**. It asks:

What are you resonating with?

Are you aligned with harmony, or caught in dissonance?

To practice temperance is to become a conscious composer of your vibrational field. By choosing peace, gratitude, and love, we contribute to the healing music of the universe.

Harmony and balance are not destinations; they are **frequencies** we choose and sustain. Every thought and action is a note in the song of our lives. Let it be a song of stillness, beauty, and divine becoming.

The Middle Way

In stillness I find sacred ground,
Where fire and water blend without sound.
No rush, no force, just ebb and flow,
Becoming all I'm meant to know.

Journaling Prompts:

1. Where do I need more balance in my life?

2. How can I blend opposites within me into harmony?

3. What "alchemy" is being created in me now?

Guided Meditation:

An angel pours water between two cups endlessly. You step into the flow, feeling balance wash over you. Affirm: *"I live in harmony with all that is."*

Chapter 20

The Devil Within: Breaking the Bonds of Fear

In Tarot, **The Devil**—number XV in the Major Arcana—is not just a symbol of darkness or evil, but a profound mirror reflecting the **unacknowledged aspects of the self**. Often misunderstood, this card represents **bondage through illusion**—the chains we wear, forged by fear, addiction, limiting beliefs, and unconscious attachments. Yet, within its daunting image lies a powerful invitation: **to awaken, confront the shadow, and reclaim our inner freedom.**

Facing the Shadow: What the Devil Reveals

When The Devil appears in a reading, it often points to **entrapment by unhealthy patterns** or unconscious desires that dominate our thoughts and actions. It urges us to ask: *Where in my life am I giving away my power?*

Negative Aspects:

- **Addiction and Obsession:** Symbolizes compulsive behaviors, from substance use to toxic relationships and over-identification with materialism.

- **Negative Thought Patterns:** Reflects limiting beliefs, chronic fear, or shame that distort our perception and dampen our potential.

- **Manipulation and Control:** May point to being controlled—or controlling others—through fear, dependency, or deception.

- **Feeling Trapped:** Suggests bondage not by external chains, but by internal fears and unresolved wounds.

Positive Potential:

- **Shadow Integration:** Invites conscious exploration of the repressed or denied parts of the self for healing and wholeness.

- **Empowered Desire:** Affirms the sacredness of desire when expressed mindfully, not compulsively.

- **Breaking Free:** Offers a path of liberation through self-awareness, courage, and responsibility.

- **Catalyst for Transformation:** When faced, The Devil can ignite profound personal evolution.

The Devil in Numerology and Astrology

Numerological Significance (XV → 6):

The Devil is card **15**, which reduces to **6**—the same number as **The Lovers** card. This link highlights **choice**, especially in relation to love, desire, and values. While

The Lovers uplift conscious, soul-based connection, The Devil exposes where we unconsciously **attach, obsess, or avoid choice altogether.**

This duality presents us with a fork in the road:

Will we continue feeding our shadow desires, or **transform them into light?**

Astrological Influence – Capricorn & Saturn:

The Devil is associated with **Capricorn**, ruled by **Saturn**, the planet of structure, limitation, and discipline. On one hand, Saturn represents the very **boundaries** that can make us feel stuck. But on the other, it offers the **tools of mastery**—discipline, realism, and inner strength—to overcome those limitations.

Capricorn energy emphasizes ambition, perseverance, and responsibility. Thus, The Devil not only shows where we are bound, but how we might **climb out of that bondage with awareness and discipline.**

The Devil as Psychological Symbol – A Jungian Lens

In **Jungian psychology**, The Devil corresponds to the **shadow archetype**—the unconscious parts of ourselves we disown or suppress. This is not necessarily evil, but rather the raw, often misunderstood aspects of our psyche: unexpressed rage, hidden desires, shame, lust, and fear.

Key Concepts:

- **The Shadow:** Composed of repressed traits, often inherited from childhood conditioning and societal expectations.

- **Not Pure Evil:** The devil within can be a force for awakening when brought to consciousness.

- **Agent of Change:** Confronting the shadow reveals truths that can lead to personal growth and individuation.

- **Individuation:** Integrating the shadow is essential in becoming a whole, authentic individual.

By facing the inner devil—not with judgment, but with **compassionate awareness**—we transmute fear into power, and bondage into liberation.

Addiction to Fear and Worry

In the modern psyche, one of the most insidious devils we face is **worry**—a socially accepted addiction rooted in fear and the illusion of control. Chronic anxiety distances us from the present moment and erodes our vitality. Like The Devil card, worry binds us with invisible chains.

But here lies the paradox: those chains are **loose**. They can be slipped off, if we choose. Through **mindfulness, surrender, and spiritual trust**, we stop feeding the fear and start aligning with the calm presence of being. The Devil, once acknowledged, becomes a doorway to deep peace.

In Essence

The Devil is not your enemy—it is your **unexamined self**. It is every unspoken fear, every repressed desire, every avoidance, projection, and coping mechanism wrapped in illusion. And yet, it also holds the **key to your liberation**. To look into The Devil's eyes is to confront the part of you that believes you're unworthy, unloved, or powerless—and to lovingly reclaim that part with compassion and sovereignty.

This card is a wake-up call. Not to fear evil, but to stop fearing yourself.

Chains Made of Smoke

The devil is not horned or red,
But whispers softly in your head.
"You're not enough," it likes to say,
And leads your truth a breath away.

But turn and face what hides in fear,
You'll find your chains were never near.
They're made of smoke, not iron or flame,
And you were always free to change.

Journaling Prompts:

1. What attachments or habits keep me bound?

2. How do I mistake illusion for freedom?

3. How can I reclaim my true power?

Guided Meditation:

You see chains around your wrists. The Devil laughs, but you realize the chains are loose. You lift them off easily. Affirm: *"I am free from illusions that bind me."*

Chapter 21

The Tower's Fall: A Sacred Unraveling

In Tarot, **The Tower**—card XVI in the Major Arcana—is often one of the most feared and misunderstood symbols. It speaks of **sudden upheaval, chaos, and destruction**, yet behind its lightning strike lies the power of profound **liberation and truth**. The Tower does not destroy for the sake of cruelty; it dismantles what is false, stagnant, or built on shaky foundations so that something more authentic may rise from the ruins.

It is a sacred unraveling—violent in appearance, but divine in intention.

Key Themes of The Tower

- **Sudden Upheaval:**

  Like a bolt of lightning, The Tower signals unexpected change—events that feel disruptive but serve to wake us from illusion or complacency.

- **Destruction of Falsehoods:**

  Whether in the form of outdated beliefs, false identities, or unstable relationships, The Tower shakes loose what can no longer be sustained.

- **Liberation and Revelation:**

  While the fall may be painful, it also frees us from entrapments we may not have seen or acknowledged. Truth, however jarring, becomes a path to freedom.

- **Catalyst for New Beginnings:**

  Once the dust settles, we are left with space—a sacred emptiness in which something new and true can take root.

- **Resistance and Suffering:**

  The card warns: the more we resist necessary change, the more forceful its arrival may be. Surrendering to transformation often eases the impact.

Numerology and Astrology of the Tower

- **Number 16 (1 + 6 = 7):**

  In numerology, **16** suggests karmic lessons and spiritual purification—often through ego collapse. Reduced to **7**, it aligns with **spiritual awakening**, introspection, and inner truth.

- **Mars Influence:**

  Astrologically, The Tower is ruled by **Mars**, the planet of action, aggression, and upheaval. Mars breaks what is rigid to clear the path for new growth.

- **Scorpio and Aries:**

  Scorpio represents **transformation and death of the old**, while Aries offers **raw force, courage, and rebirth**. Together, they echo The Tower's message: breakdown is often the beginning of breakthrough.

The Tower in Jungian Psychology:

In Jungian terms, The Tower represents the dramatic collapse of the **ego's defenses**. It is the moment when our constructed identity—often based on avoidance, pride, or false security—is shattered by the unconscious.

- **Destruction and Rebirth:**

  Like the mythic Tower of Babel, The Tower falls when we try to elevate ourselves through illusion. The collapse invites a return to authenticity and soul.

- **Confronting the Shadow:**

  The fall forces us to face what we've hidden. Repressed fears, unmet needs, and the shadow self all surface, demanding integration.

- **Individuation:**

  This chaos, painful as it may be, becomes a vital step in the process of **becoming whole**—a necessary dismantling before rebirth.

- **The Awakening Archetype:**

  The Tower is not a punishment. It is an **awakening**. A flash of lightning that shows us what was always there but unseen.

- **Jung's Bollingen Tower:**

  Ironically, Carl Jung built a literal tower—his **Bollingen Tower**—as a space for solitude, reflection, and integration of the unconscious. This structure contrasts the tarot's crumbling Tower, yet together they form a symbolic spectrum: what collapses without must be rebuilt within.

The Blessing in the Breakdown

Life is chaotic. It unravels. We lose relationships, roles, beliefs, and identities. Sometimes all at once. The Tower appears not to destroy us, but to **strip us bare of illusion**—to force us to look at what is real, raw, and unavoidably true.

There is a deeper intelligence behind these disruptions. We may not see it in the moment, but with time we often recognize that the breakdown was a **sacred initiation**—a clearing of what no longer serves, and a call to rebuild from the soul outward.

From Perfection to Presence

We often chase control, order, and perfection to feel safe. But human life, like divine design, is inherently imperfect. In our flaws, in our cracks, and in our unraveling, there is beauty. There is art. There is authenticity.

True connection comes not from polished surfaces but from **vulnerability, messiness, and shared humanity**. The Tower doesn't just tear down—it calls us back into presence. It invites **realness over performance**, truth over illusion, and grace over ego.

In Essence

The Tower card reminds us that destruction is often the beginning of **truth**, that collapse is a call to **rebirth**, and that chaos can be **sacred**. The tower falls so the soul can rise.

What falls away was never truly you. What remains becomes your foundation.

Sacred Ruins

Lightning cracks the sky so wide,
And all you've built now breaks inside.
But in the ash, a seed is sown,
Of truths you now must call your own.

Let every stone that's torn apart,
Reveal the shape of your true heart.
The Tower falls—but do not fear,
The soul you are begins right here.

Journaling Prompts:

1. What structures in my life are crumbling?

2. How does destruction make way for freedom?

3. What truth is being revealed through upheaval?

Guided Meditation:

Stand before a tower struck by lightning. As it falls, you walk through the dust — free at last. The sky clears with stars. Affirm: *"I welcome awakening through change."*

Chapter 22

The Star: Guiding Light of Destiny

In the darkest night, when all seems lost, a single star can illuminate the path ahead. The Star card in the tarot is that beacon—it shines with quiet promise, whispering of renewal, divine alignment, and the luminous possibilities that await us. A symbol of hope and healing, The Star arrives when we are ready to remember who we truly are beneath the scars of experience.

The Light After the Storm

Following the upheaval of The Tower, The Star enters like a breath of stillness after chaos. It calls us to pause, to listen, and to realign with our deeper truth. No longer clouded by illusions, we begin to trust in a higher rhythm. Where there was once disillusionment, we now find clarity. Where pain lingered, the light of healing begins to glow.

The Star teaches that renewal is not just possible—it is destined. Through grace and surrender, we enter a time of emotional healing, forgiveness, and restoration. It is a sacred reminder that our wounds, once embraced, can become wells of wisdom.

Hope as a Frequency

Hope is more than an emotion—it is a vibration. When we embody hope, we align with the universal current of life that is always moving toward expansion and love. The Star asks us to tune our internal compass to this frequency. It is the inner knowing that we are being guided, even when the path ahead is unclear.

It invites us to trust:

- In ourselves

- In the unfolding

- And in the divine intelligence that orchestrates every moment

Even in the void, The Star reminds us that the cosmos holds us. That our light—however dimmed—is never extinguished.

Astrology, Numerology, and Divine Alignment

The Star is traditionally linked to **Aquarius**, a sign associated with cosmic vision, humanitarianism, and intuitive insight. Aquarius pours divine water into both the earth and the stream—symbolizing the flow of higher knowledge into the material and emotional realms. This celestial influence emphasizes The Star's role in awakening the collective through individual illumination.

Numerologically, The Star is the 17th card of the Major Arcana (1 + 7 = 8), linking it to themes of **infinity, balance, and manifestation**. The number 8 vibrates with the energy of inner strength, karmic alignment, and the power to bring dreams into form through spiritual intention.

Together, these correspondences suggest that The Star represents a cosmic checkpoint:

A moment when soul, psyche, and destiny converge to initiate transformation.

The Star in Jungian Psychology

Carl Jung often spoke of the **"star in man"**—a divine spark nestled in the depths of the unconscious, waiting to be remembered. In dreams, stars are archetypal symbols of the Self: the unified, whole aspect of our being that transcends ego and integrates all polarities.

When a star appears in one's psyche—whether through dreams, meditation, or synchronicities—it often marks the beginning of the individuation journey. It is an inner call to authenticity, wholeness, and conscious evolution. Jungian astrologers may see the star as both a literal celestial influence and a metaphor for the soul's guiding light—one that leads us beyond illusion and into truth.

Spiritual Healing and Sacred Rebirth

Our life path is not linear—it is **spiral**, mirroring the cosmic dance of the galaxies. Healing, too, follows this sacred geometry. As we circle through layers of grief, remembrance, forgiveness, and rebirth, The Star becomes both compass and sanctuary.

It teaches that:

- Healing begins with **awareness**

- Deepens through **forgiveness**

- Culminates in a **spiritual rebirth**

True healing is holistic. It integrates body, mind, and soul through practices like prayer, energy work, meditation, ancestral healing, and conscious surrender. The Star encourages us to look not only within, but also beyond—to the **morphic fields** of collective memory where old patterns can be dissolved and new timelines awakened.

By healing our personal stories, we contribute to the healing of the whole. Each individual restoration adds light to the cosmic field—a constellation of conscious beings remembering their origin and destiny.

Reflection:

"You are not lost. You are becoming.

What you seek is already seeking you.

Follow the shimmer within—the star of your own becoming."

Whispers of the Star

A light above, so soft, so true,
It shines to guide the path for you.
When all feels lost and dreams grow far,
Look within—there burns your star.

It speaks of hope, of healing grace,
A sacred calm, a quiet place.
Through darkest night or deepest scar,
You're always held by your own star.

Journaling Prompts:

1. What gives me hope when I feel lost?

2. How do I connect to divine inspiration?

3. Where am I being called to shine my light?

Guided Meditation:

You kneel by a pool under starlight. One-star shines brightest, beaming into your heart. You drink from the water and feel renewed. Affirm: *"I am guided by the light of hope."*

Chapter 23

The Moon: Shadows of the Soul

The Moon card, the eighteenth in the Major Arcana, invites us into a realm of shadows, dreams, and the subconscious. This is not the realm of logic or daylight certainty, but of silvery illusions and intuitive truths. It signals a time of uncertainty, where clarity is veiled and things are not always what they seem. Yet within that mystery lies profound potential for inner growth, creative vision, and spiritual depth.

The Language of Symbols

The Moon symbolizes illusion and deception, not to mislead, but to urge discernment. Beneath its glow, reality distorts—dangers may lurk in unseen places, and hidden fears rise from the depths of the psyche. But this is also a time of heightened sensitivity. The Moon awakens intuition and the inner voice, calling us to navigate not by sight, but by feeling. It offers a sacred invitation: descend into the unknown, listen to your dreams, and embrace the mystery that stirs beneath the surface.

Creative Depth and Feminine Power

The Moon is also a gateway to the divine feminine, to the cyclic and receptive aspects of the psyche. It is the realm of creativity, imagination, and nonlinear knowing. It encourages us to honor emotional tides, intuitive nudges, and the symbolic language of dreams. Under its influence, artists and mystics alike receive visions that transcend logic. Here, the rational yields to the soulful, and the invisible becomes more real than the seen.

Numerology and Astrology of the Moon

Number 18 reduces to 9 (1 + 8), symbolizing spiritual completion, universal love, and the culmination of inner cycles. Astrologically, the Moon card resonates with **Pisces**, a sign ruled by **Neptune**, the planet of dreams, mysticism, and illusion. The water element deepens its emotional and subconscious themes, urging surrender to what cannot be controlled, only felt and known through intuition.

Jungian Lens: Lunar Consciousness and Ego Death

In Jungian psychology, the Moon is the archetype of the **unconscious mind**—a space of instinct, emotion, and repressed material. It is in this liminal space where ego-death occurs, where the familiar dissolves and we confront our inner darkness. The Moon's cycles—waxing, full, waning, and new—mirror our inner transformation. The **full moon** amplifies unconscious contents, while the **new moon** initiates new beginnings and reflection. In Jung's alchemical view, the Moon corresponds to the **albedo** stage—the cleansing illumination before the full realization of the Self in the solar "gold" stage.

Alchemy, Balance, and Inner Integration

Alchemy teaches that the Moon's white light cleanses and prepares the soul. But balance is key. Just as Jung emphasized the necessity of integrating the Moon's unconscious with the Sun's consciousness, so too must we harmonize feeling with clarity, surrender with awareness. The Moon without the Sun becomes chaos; the Sun without the Moon becomes dry rationality. Together, they birth wholeness.

Quantum Consciousness: Leaping Through Illusions

Extending into quantum thought, the Moon's domain aligns with the concept of **quantum jumping**—the conscious act of shifting one's reality through focused thought, imagination, and vibrational alignment. In a world shaped by illusions and false paradigms, the Moon card reminds us that reality is not fixed. Through surrender, visualization, and inner clarity, we can "jump" into timelines that align with our soul's frequency. We are not merely passive dreamers; we are **active architects** of possibility.

Concluding Reflection

The Moon beckons us not to fear the dark, but to explore it with reverence. It teaches that confusion is not failure, but a prelude to deeper knowing. When clarity fades, intuition becomes our compass. When the path disappears, imagination carves a new one. In its shadows, we are not lost—we are **initiated.**

To walk with the Moon is to walk with mystery, to face the illusions of ego and society, and to reclaim the intuitive, imaginative, and infinite nature of our soul. It is not a warning, but a whisper:

"You are more than what you see. Trust the unseen. Walk with the light inside."

Under the Moonlight

In shadows deep, where silence sings,
The Moon reveals forgotten things.
A mirror to the soul's own tide,
Where fear and wonder both reside.

She beckons soft, with silver hue,
To trust the path that feels most true.
Though veiled the road, and dim the way,
The heart knows what the mind can't say.

Journaling Prompts:

1. What illusions might be clouding my vision?

2. What do my dreams reveal to me?

3. How can I trust intuition over fear?

Guided Meditation:

You walk under moonlight, two wolves howling nearby. The path winds mysteriously, but you listen to your inner voice guiding you safely onward. Affirm: *"I trust my intuition through the shadows."*

Chapter 24
The Sun: Light Beyond Shadows

The Sun card in tarot, the XIX of the Major Arcana, radiates joy, success, vitality, and illumination. It is the archetype of positivity, clarity, and personal growth. Its light dissolves confusion, bringing understanding and optimism. Yet, like the noonday sun, its brilliance can sometimes overwhelm—leading to inflated ego, unrealistic expectations, or a tendency to overlook shadows that still require integration.

Key Meanings

- **Positivity and Happiness**: The Sun shines with radiant joy, optimism, and a childlike sense of wonder.

- **Success and Achievement**: It heralds triumph in endeavors—whether in relationships, career, or personal goals.

- **Clarity and Illumination**: Hidden truths come to light, allowing deeper understanding and perspective.

- **Vitality and Energy**: It signifies vibrant health and a renewed life force.

- **Innocence and Playfulness**: The child on horseback reminds us to return to openness, simplicity, and play.

- **Shadow Aspects:** When unbalanced, it can reflect being blinded by optimism, ignoring warning signs, or clinging to appearances.

Love and Relationships

- **New Beginnings and Joy:** The Sun heralds passion, intimacy, and playful connection.

- **Healthy Self-Esteem:** It affirms relationships grounded in mutual respect and wholeness.

- **Shadow in Love:** Its warmth may tempt us to gloss over challenges or neglect the deeper needs of a partner.

- **For the Single:** It encourages boldness, flirtation, and the confidence to express love openly.

Astrological and Numerological Resonance

- **Astrology:** The Sun itself is the ruler of ego, vitality, and identity. Its zodiac counterpart is **Leo**, a sign of confidence, generosity, and creative expression.

- **Numerology:** As card XIX, the Sun embodies both completion and renewal. Reduced to 1 (1+9=10, 1+0=1), it connects to **The Magician**, highlighting manifestation, self-discovery, and the power of new beginnings.

Jungian Archetype of the Sun

In Jungian psychology, the Sun symbolizes **consciousness and the Self**—the radiant center of our being. Its rising parallels the dawn of life; its zenith, the fullness of maturity; its setting, the wisdom of introspection. As an archetype, the Sun illuminates truth, awakens awareness, and guides individuation—the journey toward wholeness.

It also exists in dynamic relationship with its opposite, the Moon. Where the Moon embodies the unconscious and mystery, the Sun represents clarity and rational light. Together, they mirror the balance between shadow and illumination, unconscious and conscious, feminine and masculine.

Spiritual and Soulful Meaning

On the soul's journey, the Sun signifies **awakening into the truth of one's essence**. Its light pierces through illusion, fear, and shame, revealing authenticity and divine purpose. It ignites creative power and reminds us of our role as co-creators—artists of light shaping form and weaving heaven into earth.

In this state of radiance, life transcends survival. We thrive. Every action becomes intentional; every moment infused with joy. Illusions are recognized as lessons rather than prisons, and the chains of limitation dissolve into wings of freedom.

Concluding Narrative

The Sun is not just a symbol of joy—it is the living force of awakening, reminding us that illumination transforms, not just informs. It reveals our truest self, frees us from shadow, and aligns us with divine purpose. To walk in the light of the Sun is to embody vitality, clarity, and authenticity, thriving as radiant expressions of the soul. It teaches that when we embrace life with openness, play, and courage, we no longer merely exist— we shine.

Radiance Unveiled

The light breaks through, dissolving night,
A song of joy, a soul's birthright.
No shadow binds, no fear can stay,
The Sun reveals the brighter way.

Alive, we shine, our hearts set free,
Creators of divine decree.
With open hands, our truth begun,
We live, we love—we are the Sun.

Journaling Prompts:

1. Where in my life do I feel most joyful?

2. What "inner child" qualities am
   I reclaiming?

3. How do I radiate light to others?

Guided Meditation:

Ride a white horse under the shining sun. A child within you laughs with pure joy. The warmth fills your whole being. Affirm: *"I shine with joy, clarity, and vitality."*

Chapter 25
Judgement: The Sacred Reckoning

The Judgment card in Tarot signifies rebirth, awakening, and transformation. It heralds the close of one cycle and the dawning of another, inviting reflection and conscious choice. At its core, this card represents a spiritual call—a summons to rise into alignment with your higher self and embrace a new chapter of life with integrity and purpose.

Key Meanings

- **Rebirth and Renewal** – The card often appears when you are ready to release the past and step into a new beginning.

- **Spiritual Awakening** – It signals a moment of clarity, when truth pierces through illusions, awakening you to your higher potential.

- **Decision-Making** – Judgment calls for pivotal choices that may alter the course of your path.

- **Self-Reflection** – It urges you to examine past actions honestly, to make amends, and to move forward with wholeness.

- **Inner Calling** – The card asks you to listen to the wisdom of your soul and trust your intuitive guidance.

Reversed, Judgment may indicate hesitation, self-doubt, or the resistance to change. It can suggest missed opportunities, fear of judgment, or delays in making necessary choices.

In Readings

The Judgment card often appears at turning points—whether in career, relationships, or spiritual growth. It indicates profound shifts that carry lasting consequences.

For example, in love, Judgment may signify renewal in a relationship or the courage to embrace a new chapter together. In all contexts, it calls for honesty, accountability, and faith in transformation.

Astrological and Numerological Correspondences

- **Pluto:** Judgment is associated with Pluto, planet of transformation and rebirth. Its influence highlights endings, regeneration, and the power of awakening through surrender.

- **Number 20 (reducing to 2):** The number 20 symbolizes awakening and higher calling, while its reduction to 2 emphasizes balance, harmony, and partnership. Together, they remind us that transformation often unfolds in the mirror of relationship—whether with others, with life, or with the self.

Jungian Psychology

In Jungian thought, the Judgment card represents spiritual awakening and the integration of shadow. It is the moment of reckoning when one confronts hidden patterns and accepts responsibility for past choices. Through this confrontation comes liberation, a shedding of outdated identities, and the courage to live authentically.

The archetypal resonance is one of **resurrection**—an emergence from the depths of the unconscious into the clarity of higher awareness. It is both a personal and collective awakening, calling us to shed illusions and step into the truth of our being.

The Inner Journey

Awakening begins when the soul questions the constructs that once defined its reality. Subtle at first—a whisper within—it deepens through self-inquiry, reflection, and the healing of ancestral and collective wounds. Each layer of conditioning shed is a step closer to the divine spark within, which has always known its infinite worth.

This journey is not about gaining, but about **unlearning and unbecoming**. We reclaim the scattered fragments of our soul once surrendered for acceptance or love. As illusions dissolve, we move from an outward-driven existence to an inwardly guided life. In this state, truth cannot be ignored—and once known, it transforms everything.

Like light breaking through fog, truth illuminates the hidden corners of the psyche. It does not merely inform—it liberates. Fear and shame give way to authenticity. The soul, radiant and alive, takes its rightful place as co-creator of reality, shaping life with love, wisdom, and divine intention.

Concluding Narrative

The Judgment card is a sacred call to rise. It is the trumpet that awakens the sleeping soul, a reminder that every ending carries within it a new beginning. It asks us to stand in truth, to release the weight of the past, and to step forward renewed, reborn, and aligned with divine purpose.

Through this reckoning, we realize that judgment is not condemnation, but liberation. It is the moment we reclaim our light and remember that we are eternal beings, radiant with the power to create heaven on earth through the vibration of love.

The Call of Truth

A trumpet sounds, the veil is torn,
From shadow's sleep, the soul reborn.
The past dissolves, its weight released,
Awakening calls, the heart finds peace.

No chains remain, no lies conceal,
The light within begins to heal.
Through sacred fire, we rise anew,
In love, in truth—our souls shine through.

Journaling Prompts:

1. What "old self" am I ready to release?

2. What inner calling is summoning me now?

3. How can I rise into my higher purpose?

Guided Meditation:

Hear a trumpet sounding. Graves open, and souls rise upward. You too rise, shedding old identities. A voice within calls: *"Awaken, it is time."* Affirm: *"I answer the call of my soul."*

- **Wholeness and Integration**

  The card represents the weaving together of experiences and lessons into a cohesive whole.

- **Celebration and Joy**

  It is often accompanied by a sense of festivity, marking milestones or sacred thresholds in life.

- **Transition and Renewal**

  Though it closes one cycle, the World always ushers in new beginnings, preparing the soul for its next adventure.

Upright vs. Reversed

- **Upright:** Harmony, completion, and successful outcomes. Life feels aligned and whole.

- **Reversed:** Delays, incompletion, or stagnation—suggesting obstacles must be addressed before true closure arrives.

Applications in Context

- **Love:** A milestone in relationship growth or a deep sense of self-fulfillment in love's pursuit.

- **Career:** Successful achievements, professional culmination, or opportunities for global reach and recognition.

Astrological and Numerological Layers

- **Astrology:** The World is linked with **Jupiter**, planet of expansion, wisdom, and fortune, reinforcing its themes of abundance and growth.

- **Zodiac:** The four figures—man, lion, bull, and eagle—represent Aquarius, Leo, Taurus, and Scorpio, symbolizing balance of all elements and the cycle's completion.

- **Numerology:** As **XXI** (21), the card represents culmination and fulfillment. Twenty-one, a sacred trinity of sevens, is tied to completion, mastery, and success.

Jungian Psychology: Individuation Complete

In Jungian thought, the World symbolizes the **completion of individuation**—the process of integrating all aspects of the psyche into a unified Self.

- **The Fool's Journey:** From innocence to wisdom, the Fool's adventure finds its completion in the World, where all lessons converge.

- **Wholeness:** Integration of archetypes and experiences leads to inner and outer harmony.

- **The Self:** The World mirrors Jung's archetype of the Self—totality, unity, and the balance of conscious and unconscious dimensions.

- **Eternal Perspective:** It points beyond time, suggesting that completion is not finality but participation in an eternal cycle of creation.

Quantum and Spiritual Perspective

The World invites us to embrace a deeper truth: reality is not fixed but fluid, shaped by perception and consciousness. Quantum physics teaches that the **observer effect** collapses infinite potential into form.

Spiritually, this reveals that we are not passive recipients of life but active creators.

Completion, therefore, is not merely an outcome of effort but an act of **unlearning**—releasing distortions, healing separations, and attuning to the frequency of truth and wholeness.

When we choose to believe and embody a reality with conviction, it materializes. The World teaches that our "realness" is born not from external events, but from conscious alignment with unity, abundance, and love.

Concluding Narrative

The **World** is not simply the end of a journey—it is the recognition that endings and beginnings are inseparable. It reminds us that wholeness is not found outside of us but discovered within, as we integrate our experiences, transcend illusions, and embrace our role as conscious creators.

It is the dance of unity, the sacred circle of life, and the eternal return to Source. In the World, the Fool has become wise, and wisdom has led back to innocence— ready to step once again into the infinite adventure of becoming.

Circle of Wholeness

The circle closes, yet opens anew,
All fragments unite, all paths come through.
In wholeness we stand, both humble and free,
The World completes what the soul came to be.

Journaling Prompts:

1. What chapter of my life feels complete now?

2. Where do I feel most in harmony with the Universe?

3. How do I honor both endings and new beginnings?

Guided Meditation:

Stand within a wreath of light, the four guardians surrounding you. You dance with freedom and grace. All your experiences weave together. Affirm: *"I am whole, complete, and ready for the next journey."*

Closing Reflection: The Fool's Map of Wholeness

The Journey Comes Full Circle

The Fool's path is not a straight line, but a sacred spiral. Each step through the Major Arcana has guided you into deeper aspects of self: the power to manifest, the wisdom of intuition, the strength of surrender, the liberation of transformation, and finally, the wholeness of integration.

To walk the Fool's path is to live in constant awakening, always beginning, always expanding, always remembering that every ending is but another beginning.

Integrative Journaling Prompts

1. Which Major Arcana archetype do I feel most aligned with right now, and why?

2. Which archetype challenges me the most, and what lesson does it carry for me?

3. Looking back, how has my own life mirrored the Fool's journey of growth, trial, and transformation?

4. If I were to draw a new card beyond *The World*, what would it symbolize in my ongoing journey?

Guided Meditation: The Circle of the Fool

Close your eyes and imagine walking along a vast spiral path. As you walk, each archetype you have met — Magician, High Priestess, Empress, Emperor, and all the others — appear one by one. Each blesses you with a gift: wisdom, courage, compassion, clarity. At last, you arrive at the center of the spiral, where the Fool stands smiling, holding out their hand.

You take their hand, and suddenly you see — the Fool was you all along. The journey was never about reaching a destination, but about remembering your wholeness.

Whisper aloud:

"I am the Fool, ever beginning, ever becoming, ever whole."

Part III

Integration and Transformation

Chapter 27
The Fool's Return – Circle of Wholeness

Introduction: The Eternal Return

In both spirituality and the Tarot, the concept of "ending as a new beginning" reflects one of the most profound truths of human existence: nothing ever truly ends, it merely transforms. Seasons shift, relationships evolve, and identities dissolve only to be reborn in new forms. This is not a simple cycle that endlessly repeats itself, but a spiral that carries us upward into ever-expanding levels of consciousness.

The Fool, numbered 0 in the Tarot, embodies the boundless potential of beginnings. The Death card, often misunderstood, represents the shedding of the old so that something new can be born. Together, they illustrate the paradoxical truth: only by embracing endings can we step into new beginnings. In life, we are constantly invited to become the Fool again—innocent, open, and ready to take a leap of faith—while carrying with us the wisdom of all our past journeys.

Spiritual practices such as journaling, meditation, and Tarot contemplation help us recognize this spiral of transformation. They remind us that growth is rarely linear. Instead, we are guided to revisit familiar themes—

love, fear, authority, surrender, hope—each time from a more elevated perspective. With each revolution of the spiral, our consciousness deepens, our compassion widens, and our ability to integrate lessons grows stronger.

The Fool's return to the World and beyond symbolizes this **circle of wholeness.** Having danced through every archetype of the Major Arcana, the Fool does not simply end; he begins again, carrying both innocence and wisdom into the next turn of the spiral.

Understanding the Concept of Spiritual Transformation

Spiritual Context

Life is not a straight road with a beginning and an end. It is a dance of cycles—birth and death, creation and dissolution, rising and falling. Every ending is a threshold. When a chapter closes, whether it is the loss of a job, the end of a relationship, or the conclusion of a personal phase, it opens the possibility of something new. The deeper purpose of spirituality is to teach us to recognize these thresholds not with fear but with reverence.

To see an ending as a finality is to misunderstand the soul's journey. To see it as a doorway is to recognize life's ever-renewing nature. The spiritual seeker learns to embrace change, even painful change, as necessary compost for the flowering of new life.

Tarot in Context

The Tarot cards are mirrors of these truths.

- **The Death card** symbolizes not physical death but transformation, renewal, and the completion of a cycle. It invites us to let go of what no longer serves, even if clinging feels safer.

- **The Fool** represents trust, openness, and the willingness to leap into the unknown. With each cycle's end, the Fool appears again, asking us: "Will you trust life enough to step forward into the mystery?"

- **The tens in the Minor Arcana**—Ten of Cups, Ten of Wands, Ten of Pentacles, Ten of Swords—represent culminations in the realms of emotion, action, materiality, and thought. But each culmination is also an invitation to continue the journey, to move beyond comfort zones, and to embrace fresh challenges.

The Tarot does not present life as a closed loop but as an evolving spiral where every ending bears the seed of a new beginning.

Navigating Transitions

Embracing Change

Change is the only constant. Yet it is often the most resisted. The ego prefers stability, familiarity, and predictability. But spiritual transformation demands that we surrender to impermanence. Just as a caterpillar must dissolve into formlessness before becoming a butterfly, so must we undergo moments of disintegration to discover our truer forms.

The Tarot teaches us that painful endings are not punishments but initiations. The Tower may crumble, Death may strip away illusions, but these very upheavals clear space for the birth of a new consciousness.

Processing the Past

One of the keys to navigating transitions is not to deny the past but to honor it. Journaling, meditation, or reflective Tarot spreads allow us to revisit what has been lived, not to dwell in regret, but to harvest the wisdom from experience. Each challenge, each mistake, each joy contains within it the seeds of growth.

To process the past is to transmute it—from burden into wisdom, from pain into compassion, from memory into meaning. This alchemy of the soul is the foundation of transformation.

Setting Intentions

Once the past has been honored and released, the next step is to set intentions for the new cycle. Intentions are not rigid goals but guiding lights. The Fool does not know where the road will lead, but he sets out with trust. Similarly, we do not need to control every detail of the future; rather, we need to clarify the qualities we wish to embody—peace, courage, love, creativity. Tarot spreads, meditation, or affirmations can serve as portals to articulate these intentions and align them with the soul's deeper call.

Practical Applications of Tarot for Transformation

1. **Use Tarot as a Mirror, not a Fortune-Teller**

    Instead of asking, "What will happen?" ask, "What is this moment teaching me? What must I release? What energy is seeking to emerge?" This shifts Tarot from prediction to empowerment.

2. **Embrace the Liminal Space**

    Transitions often feel like floating in-between worlds. This liminal space is uncomfortable, but it is sacred. It is the womb where the old dissolves and the new gestates. Tarot cards such as the Hanged Man remind us to surrender to these pauses, trusting that stillness itself is fertile.

3. **View Life as a Spiral**

    When the same challenges appear again, it does not mean we have failed. It means we are encountering the same theme at a higher octave. For instance, someone may repeatedly struggle with trust in relationships. Each new relationship revisits this theme, but with deeper awareness and new opportunities for healing. The spiral view transforms frustration into recognition of ongoing refinement.

The Spiral Nature of Spiritual Growth

Spiritual growth is not a straight ascent toward enlightenment. It is a spiral—ascending yet revisiting, progressive yet circular.

Key Aspects

- **Non-Linear Progression** – Growth rarely follows predictable lines. It bends, pauses, and doubles back, only to surge forward again.

- **Revisiting Old Themes** – Old wounds resurface, not to punish us, but to offer deeper healing.

- **Increased Understanding** – Each repetition brings more clarity and integration.

- **Transformation, Not Regression** – What feels like "going backward" is actually circling upward into expanded consciousness.

- **Symbol of Connection** – Spirals are found in galaxies, seashells, and DNA. They remind us that our path mirrors the universal design.

- **Gradual Refinement** – The soul's transformation unfolds slowly, sometimes across lifetimes, with each turn of the spiral polishing its radiance.

- **Growing Self-Awareness** – Each ascent demands greater honesty about motives, shadows, and intentions.

Navigating the Spiral

- **Embrace the Cycle** – Instead of resenting repeated challenges, welcome them as higher initiations.

- **Seek Deeper Insight** – Ask not "Why again?" but "What new wisdom does this familiar situation carry now?"

- **Integrate and Apply** – Wisdom must be lived, not just understood. Each lesson must translate into new actions, relationships, and service.

- **Cultivate Awareness** – The spiral invites us to greater self-honesty. By tracking patterns and motives, we prevent unconscious repetition.

- **Trust the Process** – Even when the spiral feels endless, trust that every revolution brings the soul closer to wholeness.

The Fool's Journey as a Spiral of Consciousness

The Major Arcana can be read as a map of this spiral journey, reflecting Jung's process of individuation, the integration of conscious and unconscious into a whole Self.

1. Innocence and Engagement with the World

The Fool begins in innocence, stepping into the external world with curiosity. Encounters with the Magician and High Priestess awaken the polarity of conscious will and unconscious wisdom. The Empress and Emperor represent the nurturing and structuring forces of early life, while the Hierophant introduces cultural, spiritual, and educational systems. The Lovers and the Chariot challenge the Fool to navigate relationships and personal will.

This phase builds the **ego**, a functional self that can engage with the outer world.

2. Turning Inward: Exploration of the Subconscious

At mid-journey, the Hermit calls the Fool inward. Here, reflection replaces external striving. The Wheel of Fortune reveals life's cyclical nature, while Justice demands accountability. The Hanged Man asks for surrender, leading into the transformative passage of Death.

This stage dissolves old structures, inviting the integration of the unconscious and shadow aspects of the psyche.

3. Awakening and Integration

Having faced dissolution, the Fool rises into greater wholeness. Temperance teaches balance, the Devil exposes the shadow's grip, and the Tower shakes illusions. From this breakdown, the Star brings hope, the Moon awakens imagination and fear, and the Sun radiates clarity and joy.

Judgement calls the soul to a higher Self, culminating in the World—a vision of wholeness and integration.

Repetition at Higher Levels

Yet the World is not the end. It is the threshold of another beginning. The Fool emerges again, not as naïve innocence but as conscious innocence—choosing trust even with the knowledge of pain and impermanence.

At each new spiral, the archetypes reappear, but their lessons deepen:

- The Magician's tools are wielded with greater mastery.

- The High Priestess's mysteries are received with greater humility.

- Death is no longer feared but embraced as transformation.

- The World becomes not a final destination but a resting place before another leap.

In this way, the Fool's "foolishness" transforms from childlike ignorance to enlightened trust. Each revolution of the spiral expands awareness, embodying both psychological wholeness and spiritual enlightenment.

Conclusion: Living the Circle of Wholeness

The Fool's Return is a reminder that transformation is not a single event but an eternal rhythm. Each ending, each crisis, each death—literal or symbolic—is but an invitation to step once again into the unknown with faith. The Tarot teaches us to embrace this rhythm, to honor the spiral of growth, and to trust the wisdom of our own evolving journey.

The circle of wholeness does not mean perfection. It means integration—the weaving together of light and shadow, joy and sorrow, beginning and ending. The Fool's journey calls us not to escape life but to participate in its dance with openness, courage, and love.

Guided Meditation: Returning as the Fool

Find a quiet space where you can sit comfortably. Close your eyes and take three deep, cleansing breaths.

1. **Grounding in the Present**

    Feel the earth beneath you. Imagine roots growing from your body into the ground, anchoring you in safety and support.

2. **Releasing the Past**

    Visualize a circle of light before you. Inside this circle, see images of all that you have experienced in this current cycle—the joys, the sorrows, the achievements, the losses. Breathe deeply, and with gratitude, bow to these experiences. Whisper silently: *"I honor what has been. I release it with love."*

3. **Stepping into the Unknown**

    Now imagine a doorway appearing in the circle. Beyond it lies a vast horizon of light. See yourself holding the small knapsack of the Fool—inside it are the gifts of all your past lessons. Step lightly through the doorway. Feel the fresh air of a new beginning, the spaciousness of possibility.

4.   **Embodying Trust**

As you walk forward, sense the presence of the Fool within you—innocent, joyful, open. Allow yourself to smile. With each breath, affirm silently: *"I trust the journey. I welcome the unknown."*

5.   **Integration**

Slowly bring awareness back to your body. Place your hand on your heart and whisper: *"I am whole. I am ready. I return as the Fool, carrying wisdom into new beginnings."*

Take a final deep breath, and when you feel ready, open your eyes.

Closing Reflection

The Fool's Return is not about erasing the past, but about integrating it so completely that you can step into the future without fear. Each time you return to the beginning, you do so at a higher turn of the spiral—lighter, freer, wiser. This is the essence of transformation: not escape from the cycles of life, but conscious participation in them, with trust that every step is leading you toward deeper whole

Chapter 28

Tarot as a Tool for Personal Transformation: Meditation, Journaling, and Shadow Integration

Tarot is often imagined as a tool for fortune-telling, a way to peer into the future and predict outcomes beyond our control. Yet to confine the Tarot to this narrow role is to miss its deeper potential. At its essence, Tarot is not about external prophecy but about internal revelation. It is a mirror that reflects the unconscious mind, a symbolic map of the soul's journey, and a guide that helps us access the inner wisdom already present within us. When approached intentionally, Tarot becomes a profound companion in the work of personal transformation—an ally in meditation, journaling, and shadow integration.

In this chapter, we will explore how Tarot serves as a tool for deep inner practice. We will look at meditation with the cards, journaling and dreamwork as ways of tracking growth, and the courageous journey of shadow integration. These practices are not about predicting life events but about engaging life more consciously. They invite us to step into the inner temple of the self, encounter our truths, and embrace the fullness of who we are.

Tarot and the Transformational Path

Transformation is not a single event but a lifelong unfolding. It is the process of awakening to greater awareness, shedding outdated layers of conditioning, and embracing new aspects of the self. Many spiritual traditions, from Buddhism to alchemy, speak of this journey as a cycle of death and rebirth. Tarot, with its archetypal imagery and symbolic language, maps this very process.

The **Major Arcana**, from The Fool to The World, outlines the archetypal steps of spiritual evolution. The **Minor Arcana**, through its four suits—Wands, Cups, Swords, and Pentacles—reflects the everyday challenges and lessons that shape us. When used for meditation, journaling, and shadow work, the Tarot offers us not just insights but practices: ways of engaging with our inner world, cultivating mindfulness, and integrating fragmented parts of ourselves.

1. Meditation with the Cards

Focusing on the Imagery and Symbolism

Tarot meditation begins with a simple but profound act: gazing at a card. Each card is a visual mandala, dense with archetypal imagery—figures, symbols, colors, numbers—

that speak directly to the unconscious. When we sit quietly with a card, allowing its imagery to unfold in our awareness, we are no longer analyzing with the rational mind alone; we are inviting the language of intuition and imagination to speak.

For example, meditating on **The Star** card may evoke feelings of hope, serenity, or divine guidance. By simply breathing with the image—letting the soft light of the star pour into our awareness—we create space for healing and renewal. The practice is less about intellectual interpretation and more about attunement: listening to what arises within us as we engage the symbol.

This process transforms the card from a static image into a living experience. Like a koan in Zen practice, the card becomes a focus that transcends linear thought, drawing us into presence and insight.

Active Imagination with Tarot

Carl Jung developed a method called **Active Imagination**, a way of engaging with unconscious imagery by entering it and allowing it to unfold as a living dialogue. Applied to Tarot, this means stepping into the card's scene in meditation.

Imagine, for instance, meditating on **The Hermit**. In active imagination, you might visualize yourself walking into the snowy landscape where the Hermit stands, lantern in hand. You could approach him and ask: *What* *wisdom do you carry for me?* The Hermit may speak, or you may feel his silence as an answer in itself. Perhaps he gestures to the lantern, suggesting that the light you seek has always been within you.

Such inner journeys allow unconscious material to surface—memories, emotions, forgotten longings—that can later be integrated through reflection or journaling. In this way, Tarot meditation becomes both a contemplative and therapeutic practice.

Intuition and Inner Guidance

At its heart, Tarot meditation trains us to trust our **intuition**. In a world dominated by rational analysis, intuition often goes unheard. Yet Tarot, with its symbolic richness, invites us to listen to the quieter, subtler voice within. By meditating on the cards, we strengthen this intuitive muscle.

A simple practice: draw one card each morning, meditate on its imagery for five minutes, and hold its essence in your awareness throughout the day. Notice how life reflects the card's energy back to you. Over time, this daily ritual cultivates mindfulness and attunement, turning Tarot into a compass for navigating life's complexities.

2. Journaling and Dreamwork

If meditation is about presence, journaling is about integration. Writing allows us to give shape to the intangible: the fleeting emotions, insights, and intuitions that arise in meditation or card readings. When combined with Tarot, journaling becomes a practice of dialogue between the conscious and unconscious.

Tarot as Journal Prompts

One of the simplest ways to integrate Tarot into journaling is to use the cards as **prompts**. Draw a card and write in response:

- *What does this card reflect about my current situation?*

- *How does this card mirror something within me?*

- *What message is this card offering me today?*

For instance, drawing the **Five of Swords** might prompt reflections on conflict, ego struggles, or the need to let go of a battle that no longer serves you. Writing allows these themes to emerge more fully, offering clarity and perspective.

Tracking Personal Growth and Patterns

Keeping a **Tarot journal** over time provides a map of personal growth. By recording card pulls, spreads, and interpretations, patterns emerge. Perhaps you notice that the **Tower** card appears frequently during times of transition, or that the **Empress** shows up when you are reconnecting with creativity.

These patterns highlight recurring lessons and themes in your life. More than fortune-telling, this process becomes **soul-telling**—a way of seeing how your inner world evolves over weeks, months, or years.

Dream Exploration with Tarot

Dreams are another realm of unconscious wisdom, and Tarot can serve as a bridge to this dreamworld. Before sleep, you might draw a card and place it under your pillow, inviting its archetypal energy to guide your dreams. Upon waking, you can record your dream and explore its connections to the card.

For example, if you draw **The Moon** and dream of wandering through a forest at night, you might interpret the dream as a reflection of uncertainty, illusion, or the call to trust your intuition. Tarot gives symbolic language to the dream, anchoring its meaning in a framework that you can work with consciously.

3. Using Tarot for Shadow Integration

Understanding the Shadow Self

Carl Jung's concept of the **shadow** refers to the hidden aspects of ourselves—traits, desires, or memories we repress because they are unacceptable to the ego or society. The shadow is not inherently negative; it contains both the "dark" traits we fear and the "golden" qualities we have disowned, such as creativity or power. To integrate the shadow is to reclaim wholeness.

Tarot as a Mirror to the Unconscious

Tarot is uniquely suited for shadow work because it mirrors the unconscious. Cards such as **The Devil**, **Death**, or **The Tower** often evoke discomfort, but this discomfort is a doorway. These cards reveal the very aspects of ourselves we might prefer to avoid—our attachments, fears, or illusions.

By confronting these cards in readings, we confront the shadow in ourselves. The imagery serves as a projection screen for unconscious content, allowing us to externalize it and then re-integrate it.

Integrating the Shadow

Integration begins with acknowledgment. Through Tarot spreads and reflective journaling, we can ask:

- *What part of myself am I resisting?*

- *What is the hidden gift within this shadow?*

- *How can I accept and integrate this aspect into my whole self?*

For instance, drawing the **Seven of Cups** in shadow work may reveal escapism or illusion. Journaling might uncover how we distract ourselves with fantasies to avoid present challenges. Yet it may also reveal a hidden gift: imagination, creativity, and the ability to envision new possibilities. Integration means holding both the shadow and its gift with compassion.

Specific Tarot Spreads for Shadow Work

Several spreads are designed to facilitate shadow integration:

- **The Shadow Exploration Spread**: Identifies the hidden aspect of self, its origin, and its gift.

- **The Light and Shadow Balance Spread**: Reveals how shadow and light interact within a current situation.

- **The Shadow and Self-Compassion Spread**: Guides us in meeting the shadow with understanding rather than judgment.

These spreads are not about solving problems overnight but about cultivating ongoing dialogue with the unconscious. Through repeated practice, we transform the shadow from an adversary into an ally.

The Alchemy of Tarot Practice

When meditation, journaling, and shadow work are combined, Tarot becomes a true tool of **alchemy**—a way of transforming the lead of unconsciousness into the gold of awareness. Meditation attunes us to presence, journaling integrates insight into daily life, and shadow work brings hidden aspects into wholeness.

Together, these practices remind us that Tarot is not about predicting the future but about **creating the future**—a future born from greater awareness, authenticity, and self-compassion.

The Fool's journey through the cards mirrors our own journey of transformation. Each card becomes not just an image but a teacher, each practice not just a ritual but a step toward awakening. In this way, Tarot fulfills its highest purpose: to guide us back to ourselves.

Conclusion: Embracing Wholeness through Tarot

Tarot as a tool for personal transformation invites us to see life not as random chaos but as a meaningful unfolding. Through meditation, we learn to pause and listen. Through journaling, we track our growth and give form to the inner voice. Through shadow integration, we reclaim the lost parts of ourselves and step into wholeness.

This work is not always easy. It requires courage to face the unknown, discipline to maintain practice, and compassion to embrace the shadow. Yet the rewards are profound: greater clarity, deeper self-acceptance, and a sense of connection to the archetypal patterns that shape all human lives.

Ultimately, Tarot is not about divining what will happen tomorrow but about awakening to who we are today. When we use the cards not as fortune-telling devices but as mirrors of the soul, they become sacred companions on the journey of transformation—reminding us that the answers we seek are already within us.

1. Meditation with the Cards

Guided Meditation: Entering the Card

1. Choose a card that resonates with your current state or question.

2. Sit comfortably, breathe slowly, and soften your gaze upon the card.

3. Imagine the card expanding until it becomes a doorway.

4. Step through the doorway in your mind's eye. Notice the landscape, the figures, the atmosphere.

5. Interact with what you find there. If a figure is present, ask: *What message do you have for me?*

6. Receive whatever arises — words, emotions, images. Do not judge, simply observe.

7. Before leaving, thank the figure or scene for its wisdom.

8. Step back through the doorway, see the card shrink to its normal size, and return to your body.

Integration: Write down everything you experienced — even details that seem strange. Often, the unconscious speaks in symbols that only reveal meaning over time.

2. Journaling and Dreamwork

Tarot Journaling Prompts

Use these prompts regularly, either with daily draws or intentional spreads:

- *What does this card reveal about my current emotional state?*

- *What is the lesson or gift hidden in this card's imagery?*

- *If I lived fully by this card's wisdom today, how would I act differently?*

- *What recurring themes do I see in my recent card pulls?*

- *How does this card mirror something I've experienced in dreams?*

Dream Exploration Practice

1. Before bed, shuffle your deck and draw one card. Place it under your pillow or beside your bed.

2. As you drift to sleep, repeat silently: *May this card illuminate my dreams tonight.*

3. Upon waking, write down any dream fragments, feelings, or images.

4. Reflect: How do the dream and card interact? For example, if you draw **The Moon** and dream of a labyrinth, how does the card deepen the dream's meaning about uncertainty, illusion, or intuition?

This practice turns sleep into a conscious tool for transformation.

3. Shadow Integration with Tarot

Guided Shadow Meditation

1. Choose a card that makes you

uncomfortable (e.g., The Devil, The Tower, 5 of Swords).

2. Sit with the card and breathe into the discomfort it evokes.

3. Ask yourself: *What part of me resists this energy?*

4. Visualize the figure on the card speaking directly to you. Listen without judgment.

5. End by affirming: *I accept all parts of myself. Even my shadows hold wisdom.*

Shadow Journaling Prompts

- *What qualities in others trigger me, and how might they reflect disowned parts of myself?*

- *What fear is this card asking me to confront?*

- *If I befriended this shadow, how might it empower me instead of sabotaging me?*

- *What gift might be hidden within this darkness?*

Shadow Work Spreads

1. Shadow Exploration Spread (3 cards)

- Card 1: The shadow I need to face now

- Card 2: Where this shadow originated

- Card 3: The gift this shadow offers

2. Light and Shadow Balance Spread (5 cards)

- Card 1: My conscious strengths
- Card 2: My unconscious shadow
- Card 3: How the two interact
- Card 4: What I must release
- Card 5: What I must embrace

3. Shadow and Self-Compassion Spread (4 cards)

- Card 1: The shadow within me
- Card 2: What this shadow needs
- Card 3: How I can offer compassion
- Card 4: How integration will transform me

Tip: Always close shadow readings with grounding — breathe deeply, thank yourself for courage, and journal what arose.

The Transformative Cycle

These practices — meditation, journaling, shadow spreads — form a living cycle:

- **Meditation** awakens presence.
- **Journaling** integrates insight.
- **Shadow work** reclaims hidden aspects.

When practiced together, they become a path of alchemy: the transformation of fear into strength, confusion into clarity, fragmentation into wholeness.

Final Practice: A Full Tarot Transformation Ritual

Once a month, set aside an hour for a complete Tarot practice:

1. **Meditation:** Choose a card and enter it through active imagination.

2. **Journaling:** Write what you discovered, including any symbols or emotions.

3. **Shadow Spread:** Pull cards to explore what the unconscious wants you to face this month.

4. **Dreamwork:** Place one card under your pillow that night and record your dreams in the morning.

Over time, you will see your journal become not just a record of Tarot practice, but a mirror of your soul's unfolding journey.

4. Rituals for Aligning Astrology, Numerology, and Psychology

Tarot is not an isolated system. It stands at the crossroads of many wisdom traditions: astrology, numerology, and depth psychology among them. Each of these disciplines reflects the same truth — that human beings are expressions of universal patterns. When we align Tarot with these sister sciences, our practice becomes a ritual of wholeness, connecting cosmic cycles, numerical vibrations, and psychological archetypes within our own lived experience.

Astrology and Tarot: Ritual of Celestial Alignment

Astrology and Tarot are deeply intertwined. Many of the Major Arcana correspond to astrological signs and planets: *The Magician with Mercury, The Chariot with Cancer, The Star with Aquarius.* Aligning Tarot practice with astrological timing allows us to work in harmony with cosmic rhythms.

Astrological Alignment Ritual

1. **Choose the Right Timing**: Begin by noting the current Moon phase or planetary transit. For example, during a New Moon, set intentions; during a Full Moon, seek clarity and release.

2. **Select a Corresponding Card**: Draw a card linked to that celestial energy (e.g., The Moon card during a lunar ritual, The Sun card at summer solstice).

3. **Create a Sacred Space**: Light a candle in the color associated with the planet or sign

(blue for Jupiter, red for Mars, silver for the Moon).

4. **Meditate with the Card:** Gaze at the card while reflecting on the planetary or zodiacal influence present in your life. Ask: *How does this cosmic energy wish to move through me?*

5. **Closing Action:** Write a small intention, affirmation, or release statement, and place it under the card until the next lunar cycle.

This ritual aligns personal transformation with the cosmic dance, reminding us that our inner cycles echo the rhythms of the heavens.

Numerology and Tarot: Ritual of Number Vibration

Every card in the Tarot carries a numerical vibration, from The Magician's "1" of initiation to The World's "21" of completion. Numerology teaches us that numbers are not mere quantities but archetypal energies living forces that shape our journey.

Numerological Alignment Ritual

1. **Personal Year or Month Number:** Calculate your current personal year (add your birth month + day + current year until you reduce to a single digit). For example, if you are in a personal "7" year, this is a year of introspection and wisdom.

2. **Choose a Corresponding Card:** Select the Major Arcana card with that number (7 = The Chariot, 9 = The Hermit, etc.).

3. **Set the Space:** Place seven candles, stones, or objects around the card to honor its vibration.

4. **Reflective Meditation:** Journal or meditate with the question: *What is this number teaching me this year/month? What challenges and gifts does it hold?*

5. **Action Step:** Create a small symbolic act aligned with the number. For example, in a "2" year, prioritize partnerships; in a "5" year, embrace adventure and change.

Numerology rituals remind us that we live within cycles of growth and transformation — that every year and every number brings its own lesson.

Psychology and Tarot: Ritual of Archetypal Integration

Carl Jung taught that healing comes not from rejecting parts of the psyche but from integrating them. Tarot, with its archetypes, is a perfect tool for psychological alignment — a way of befriending the Persona, Anima/Animus, Self, and Shadow.

Archetypal Integration Ritual

1. **Choose Four Archetypal Cards:**

    • Persona: A court card that represents your outward self.

    • Shadow: A card you resist or dislike.

    • Inner Guide: A Major Arcana that comforts or inspires you.

    • Self: The World card, symbolizing integration.

2. **Sacred Circle:** Place the cards in a circle on your altar or floor, representing the wholeness of the psyche.

3. **Dialogue with Each:** Meditate on each card in turn, asking: *What do you need from me? What wisdom do you offer?* Write responses in your journal.

4. **Integration Act:** End by drawing the cards together into a stack and pressing them to your heart, affirming: *I welcome all parts of myself into wholeness.*

These ritual honors the psychological dimension of Tarot, helping us integrate rather than fragment, to live more authentically.

A Unified Ritual: Aligning Cosmos, Numbers, and Psyche

For deeper transformation, these elements can be woven into one practice:

1. **Astrology**: Begin by noting the current Moon phase or planetary alignment.

2. **Numerology**: Add your personal number for the year or month.

3. **Psychology**: Choose a card that mirrors your current inner archetype.

4. **Integration**: Lay the three cards (astrological, numerological, psychological) together. Reflect: *How do these energies weave into my present moment?*

5. **Closing Ritual**: Speak an affirmation that unites them, such as:

"I align with the stars above, the numbers within, and the archetypes of my soul. I walk the path of wholeness."

This integrated ritual situates the self within the great web of life — cosmos, vibration, and psyche all working together for transformation.

Conclusion: Ritual as Living Practice

Through meditation, journaling, shadow integration, and rituals of alignment with astrology, numerology, and psychology, Tarot becomes more than a deck of cards — it becomes a living initiatory path. It guides us through inner and outer cycles, reminds us of our place in the cosmos, and helps us reclaim the fragmented pieces of the soul.

Transformation, then, is not only a matter of insight but of *practice*. Each meditation, journal entry, and ritual become a steppingstone on the Fool's path — leading us ever closer to the wholeness represented by The World.

Chapter 29

Individuation and Soul Integration

Introduction: The Call to Wholeness

Carl Jung once remarked, *"Individuation means becoming an 'individual,' and, insofar as 'individuality' embraces our innermost, last, and incomparable uniqueness, it also implies becoming one's own self."*

This deceptively simple definition encapsulates one of the deepest spiritual and psychological journeys a human being can undertake. Individuation is not about ego-fulfillment or self-aggrandizement; rather, it is about peeling back the layers of conditioning, confronting hidden aspects of the psyche, and integrating them into a balanced, authentic sense of self. It is the journey of becoming whole.

Yet, individuation is not purely psychological. When coupled with the language of the soul—the symbolic language of archetypes, dreams, myths, and Tarot imagery—it expands beyond self-realization into *soul integration*. This deeper movement unites mind, body, and spirit into alignment with a higher purpose. Soul integration is not just about wholeness in the psyche, but wholeness in being—living authentically in tune with both inner truth and universal wisdom.

The Tarot, with its archetypal structure and mythic journey of the Major Arcana, becomes a map and mirror of this process. Just as Jung saw symbols as the bridge between conscious and unconscious, Tarot provides symbols alive with meaning, guiding seekers toward individuation and soul integration.

This chapter explores how Jungian individuation and Tarot interweave into a unified path of psychological growth, shadow work, archetypal integration, and spiritual awakening.

The Foundation: Jungian Individuation

The Psyche's Architecture

For Jung, the psyche is composed of:

- **The Ego:** our conscious identity, the "I" we know and present to the world.

- **The Persona:** the mask we wear to adapt socially and professionally.

- **The Shadow:** repressed aspects of ourselves, often unconscious, that contain both destructive impulses and hidden gifts.

- **The Anima/Animus:** the inner feminine within men and inner masculine within women, representing wholeness through inner gender balance.

- **The Self:** the archetype of totality, the organizing principle of the psyche that seeks integration of all parts into wholeness.

Individuation is the process of bringing these elements into conscious awareness and harmonizing them. It is not about eradicating the Shadow or dissolving the Persona but about integrating them into a balanced psyche.

The Stages of Individuation

Figure 3 Stages of Individuation

Jung described individuation as a dynamic, lifelong process rather than a linear path. However, it often unfolds in stages:

1. **Encountering the Shadow** – facing repressed qualities, fears, and impulses.

2. **Engaging the Anima/Animus** – integrating inner masculine and feminine energies.

3. **Transcending the Persona** – moving beyond masks into authentic being.

4. **Union with the Self** – realizing the inner center of wholeness, often experienced as a numinous or spiritual event.

This journey requires courage, as it demands radical honesty with oneself and willingness to confront what has been hidden. But it also offers profound rewards: authenticity, creativity, and spiritual connection.

Tarot as a Symbolic Map of Individuation

The Tarot, particularly the **Major Arcana**, mirrors this path. The Fool's journey from card 0 to card 21 illustrates the stages of growth and transformation that parallel individuation.

- **The Fool (0)** – the innocent beginning, symbol of potential.

- **The Magician (I)** – awareness of creative will and conscious intention.

- **The High Priestess (II)** – the inner voice of intuition and the unconscious.

- **The Devil (XV)** – confrontation with the Shadow and unconscious bondage.

- **The Star (XVII)** – renewal and spiritual guidance after darkness.

- **The World (XXI)** – wholeness, integration, completion.

Through meditation, journaling, and ritual with the cards, one can actively engage in individuation. Each card becomes a mirror of the psyche, offering symbolic entry points into self-reflection and transformation.

Shadow Work: The Descent into Darkness

Understanding the Shadow

The Shadow contains all that we reject, deny, or repress within ourselves. This may include socially unacceptable impulses, unresolved traumas, hidden creativity, or unlived potentials. Often, what we hate in others is a projection of our unacknowledged Shadow.

Engaging the Shadow requires bravery. It asks us to admit, *"Yes, this too is part of me."* Only then can the energy locked in repression be released and transformed.

Tarot as a Shadow Work Tool

Certain Tarot cards illuminate shadow dynamics:

- **The Devil** – addictions, illusions, bondage to fear.

- **The Moon** – illusion, projection, the murky subconscious.

- **Death** – the necessity of transformation and letting go.

- **The Tower** – the shattering of false identities.

Working with these cards in spreads can reveal unconscious patterns. For instance, drawing the Devil might prompt reflection on attachments or fears that dominate one's choices. Journaling on these revelations transforms them from unconscious influences into conscious insights.

Shadow work through Tarot becomes not an abstract exercise but a lived, symbolic dialogue with one's inner depths.

Archetypal Integration: Meeting the Inner Gods

Archetypes in the Psyche

Jung described archetypes as universal patterns within the collective unconscious. Figures such as the Hero, the Sage, the Mother, or the Trickster shape our myths, stories, and personal dreams. They are inner gods—energies that, when integrated, enrich our lives.

Tarot Archetypes as Guides

The Major Arcana embodies these archetypes vividly:

- **The Empress** – the nurturing Mother, abundance and fertility.

- **The Emperor** – authority, structure, the Father principle.

- **The Hermit** – the Sage, inner guidance, solitude.

- **The Fool** – the eternal Child, innocence and potential.

- **The Magician** – the Creator, will and manifestation.

By consciously engaging these archetypes through Tarot meditation, individuals can recognize how these energies manifest in their lives. Do you over-identify with the Emperor (control) but neglect the Empress (nurturance)?

Do you suppress your inner Fool, losing spontaneity? Awareness allows balance.

Synchronicity and Tarot: The Language of the Soul

Jung coined the term **synchronicity** to describe meaningful coincidences—moments when inner states align with external events without causal connection. Tarot readings often function this way.

Pulling the Tower card on the day a sudden job loss occurs, or drawing the Star after a period of grief, feels synchronistic. These moments provide reassurance that one's inner and outer life are interconnected, guided by a deeper pattern.

Tarot thus becomes not fortune-telling but soul dialogue, bridging conscious and unconscious through synchronicity.

From Individuation to Soul Integration

Beyond Psychology

While individuation is primarily psychological, *soul integration* is spiritual. It expands the work of integrating the psyche into aligning with the higher self and life purpose.

Where individuation harmonizes the inner world, soul integration harmonizes the inner with the outer, the personal with the transpersonal. It is the shift from self-realization to living authentically in service of soul truth.

Steps Toward Soul Integration

1. **Embrace the Shadow** – reclaim energy locked in repression.

2. **Balance the Archetypes** – engage inner patterns consciously.

3. **Listen to Synchronicity** – trust life's symbolic language.

4. **Seek Alignment** – ask: *Am I living my deepest truth?*

5. **Embodied Wholeness** – unite body, mind, and spirit in daily life.

Soul integration is not an endpoint but a continual alignment. It is living as a conscious participant in the unfolding of one's destiny.

Figure 4 Soul Integration Steps Mandala

301

Living Wholeness Through Awareness

To live wholeness is to practice awareness. It means seeing oneself clearly, with compassion, and making choices aligned with authenticity.

Principles of Wholeness

- **Integration, Not Perfection**: Wholeness embraces imperfections as part of the story.

- **Self-Compassion**: Treating oneself with kindness during struggle.

- **Presence**: Remaining rooted in the present rather than trapped in regrets or anxieties.

- **Purpose**: Living with meaning that transcends personal ego.

Benefits of Soul Integration

- **Greater Resilience**: Wholeness equips one to face challenges with balance.

- **Authentic Living**: No longer defined by masks, one lives from true self.

- **Inner Harmony**: Integration fosters peace and unity within.

- **Spiritual Awakening**: Alignment with soul brings transcendence and sacred purpose.

Conclusion: The Fool's Return

Individuation and soul integration are not linear journeys but spirals of growth. Each descent into shadow, each confrontation with archetypes, each synchronistic encounter, deepens the soul's unfolding.

The Fool, who began the journey in innocence, returns at the World card not as the same naive wanderer but as an integrated being—whole, authentic, and aligned with spirit.

In this way, Jung's individuation and the Tarot's Fool's journey converge: both guide us toward wholeness, not as perfection, but as a living integration of all parts of self.

Soul integration is the flowering of this process. It is living with awareness, embodying truth, and shining one's unique light into the world. It is the dance of psyche and soul, where inner symbols and outer life align in sacred harmony.

Practices for Soul Integration

1. Journaling Prompts for Individuation

Meeting the Shadow

- Which traits in others trigger discomfort, irritation, or judgment in me? Could these reflect qualities of my own Shadow?

- Write about a recent situation where I reacted strongly. What hidden part of me was trying to speak through this reaction?

- If I could speak with my Shadow, what would it say it needs from me right now?

Exploring Archetypes

- Which Tarot archetype (e.g., The Empress, The Magician, The Hermit) feels most alive in my life right now?

- Which archetype do I resist or avoid? What might that resistance reveal?

- Imagine embodying a neglected archetype for a day. How would my actions and choices shift?

Authenticity and the Self

- Where in my life am I wearing a mask (Persona)?

- What would living in greater authenticity look like in my relationships, work, and inner life?

- How do I currently experience the presence of my deeper Self?

2. Tarot Spread: The Soul Integration Layout

Card 1 – The Mask: What Persona am I wearing that hides my true self?

Card 2 – The Shadow: What unconscious part of me seeks recognition?

Card 3 – The Archetype: Which inner archetypal force is most active in my journey now?

Card 4 – The Lesson: What wisdom is life offering me through synchronicity?

Card 5 – The Self: How is my higher Self calling me toward greater integration?

After drawing, journal on each card. Notice not only the imagery but also emotional reactions — they often reveal unconscious content surfacing for integration.

3. Meditation: Dialogue with the Self

Preparation: Sit in a quiet place with a Tarot card that resonates with you in this moment (perhaps The Hermit, The Star, or The World).

Steps:

1. **Breathe:** Slow your breath, centering yourself in the present.

2. **Enter the Image:** Visualize stepping into the landscape of the card. Notice colors, symbols, and the figure(s) within.

3. **Dialogue:** Approach the central figure and ask:

- "What part of me do you represent?"

  - "What do you want me to know right now?"

- "How can I embody your wisdom in my daily life?"

4. **Receive:** Allow images, words, or sensations to arise. Trust the subconscious.

5. **Return:** Step back from the card's world, carrying the insight into waking awareness.

Integration: Journal what you discovered. Notice how the message relates to current challenges or desires.

4. Daily Practice for Living Wholeness

- **Morning Check-In:** Before the day begins, pull one card. Ask: *Which aspect of myself needs attention today?*

- **Shadow Compassion:** When you notice judgment or projection, pause and ask: *Is this reflecting something unacknowledged in me?*

- **Evening Reflection**: Write down one moment when you felt most authentic today and one moment when you felt least authentic. How can you move closer to alignment tomorrow?

Closing Reflection

Individuation and soul integration are not abstract theories but lived realities. Through journaling, Tarot, meditation, and daily awareness, the seeker gradually unites shadow and light, Persona and Self, human and divine.

The Tarot becomes more than cards — it becomes a mirror of the soul and a dialogue with the unconscious. Jung's psychology, far from being confined to the clinic, becomes a living path of spiritual awakening.

The Fool, having traversed shadow and archetypes, returns transformed. And so too do we, each day that we choose wholeness over fragmentation, authenticity over masks, and awareness over unconsciousness.

Conclusion: The Eternal Fool

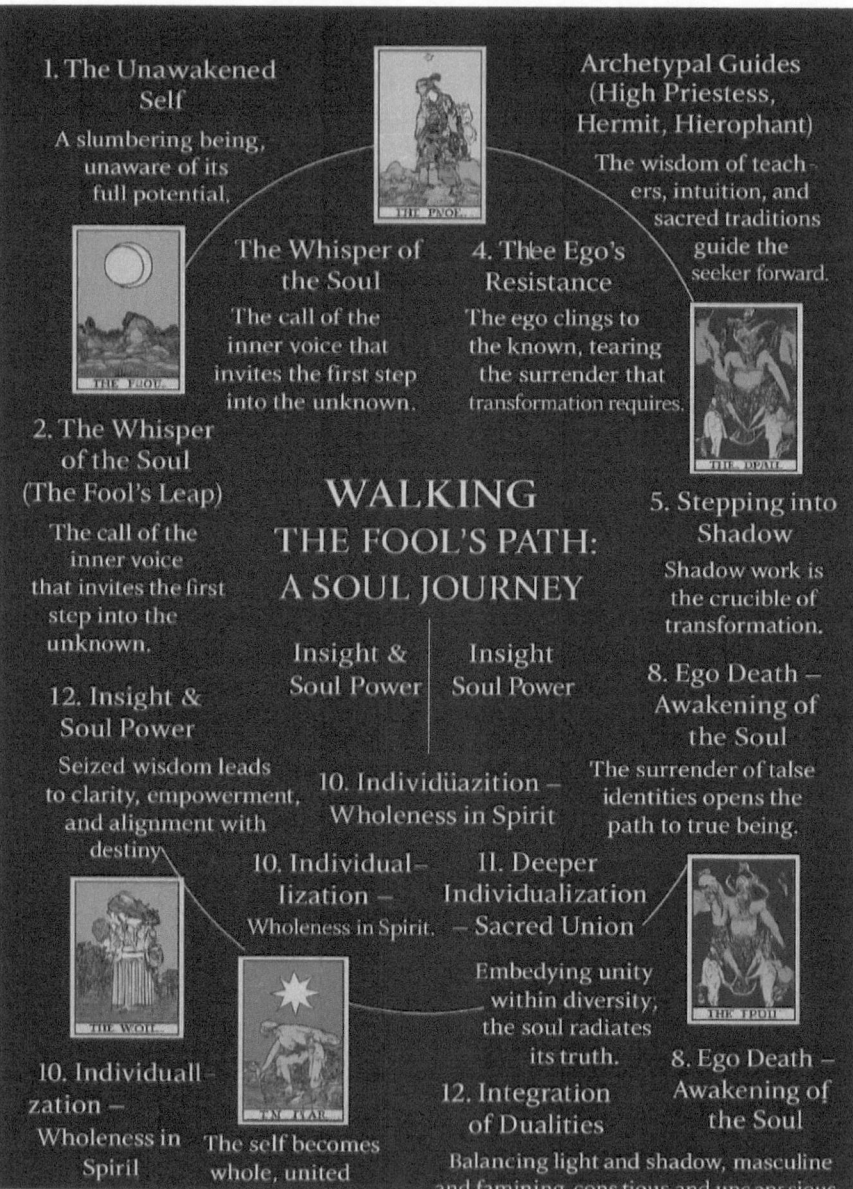

Figure 5 Walking the Fool's Path to the Soul

The Path of Wonder, Risk, and Discovery Never Ends

The Fool's journey in the Tarot begins with a leap into the unknown. Card zero, the infinite circle of beginnings, represents pure potential—the innocence of the soul before it becomes entangled in the structures of identity, society, and karma. Yet as we reach the end of the Major Arcana with *The World*, what is revealed is not a final destination, but the beginning of yet another cycle. The Fool does not vanish at the end of the story; the Fool returns, eternal, ready to leap again.

Life is not a single straight line with one victory to achieve or one wisdom to grasp. Rather, it is an unending spiral where each cycle of growth brings us closer to wholeness while simultaneously opening us to greater mystery. No matter how much we learn, achieve, or integrate, there is always another frontier of soul discovery waiting beyond the horizon.

This is why the Fool is both the first and the last. The Fool is present when a child takes their first step, when an elder breathes their last breath, and in every threshold moment between. The Fool represents the capacity to embrace uncertainty with trust, to view the unknown not as a threat but as an invitation.

When we embody the Eternal Fool, we acknowledge that wonder never fades. There is no final mastery, no permanent plateau where discovery ends. Even enlightenment itself is not an endpoint but a doorway into further unfolding. The Fool whispers to us: "Stay curious. Remain open. Walk forward with faith even when the path dissolves under your feet."

To live as the Eternal Fool is to embrace risk not as recklessness, but as the willingness to grow. Every risk is an initiation into deeper selfhood, into the truth of who we are beyond masks and fears. To leap into the unknown is to trust that the soul is carried by a current larger than the ego can grasp, a current that always leads toward wholeness—even if the way is winding.

The Fool teaches us that discovery is not reserved for the young or uninitiated; it is the essence of life itself. The oldest sages, the wisest mystics, the most advanced souls all return to the posture of the Fool again and again. For to stop leaping is to stop living.

Tarot as a Companion for Lifelong Soul Evolution

Many encounter the Tarot as a system for prediction, a way of asking "what will happen to me?" Yet, as our journey through the archetypes reveals, Tarot is less about foretelling fixed outcomes and more about illuminating the landscapes of the soul. The cards are mirrors, maps, and companions—symbols that awaken within us the recognition of where we stand on the path and what energies are asking for integration.

When approached not as fortune-telling but as a sacred dialogue, Tarot becomes a lifelong companion in soul evolution. The cards grow with us. A card pulled at age twenty will not mean the same as it does at age sixty, though the imagery is unchanged. The Fool drawn in youth may speak of reckless adventure, while the same Fool later in life may whisper of spiritual surrender. The cards reflect not only universal archetypes but also the subtle shifts of our consciousness over time.

Each return to the Tarot is an invitation to meet ourselves anew. To sit with the cards is to say: "I am open to what my soul wishes me to see today." This openness is the Fool's posture of trust—trust that guidance comes not from external forces dictating fate but from the deep alignment of our inner being with the archetypal patterns of existence.

The Major Arcana, traversed again and again, becomes a spiral staircase of growth. One year, we may be journeying through *The Tower*, dismantling illusions that no longer serve. Another year, we may bask in *The Sun*, embodying vitality and joy. And always, once *The World* has turned, the Fool greets us once more, reminding us that endings are but beginnings dressed in disguise.

Tarot is not a static book of symbols but a living companion. It listens as much as it speaks. It does not impose answers but stirs within us the capacity to discern. Its purpose is not to control destiny but to align us with it. In this sense, Tarot is less a tool and more a relationship—an intimate dialogue between soul and symbol.

As companions on the path, the cards remind us that we are never alone in our evolution. The archetypes they embody are not abstract ideas but living presences within us. To walk with Tarot is to walk with the Fool, the Magician, the High Priestess, the Hermit, and all others who mirror the facets of our own inner self.

Thus, Tarot becomes more than a deck of images; it becomes a sacred mirror of eternal companionship, us through the labyrinth of life.

Stepping Forward: Where Does Your Next Leap Call You?

The Fool does not ask us to know the entire path. In fact, the Fool insists that we cannot know. The invitation is not to certainty but to courage. The question is not "what will happen if I leap?" but "what part of me longs to leap?"

This is the essence of spiritual practice—not to escape risk but to learn to embrace it consciously. The leap may be external: a new career, a relationship, a relocation. Or it may be internal: surrendering an old identity, forgiving a wound, opening to joy. In both cases, the leap calls us beyond the known and into the potential of the soul's becoming.

To ask, "where does your next leap call you?" is to turn the Tarot outward and inward simultaneously. Outward, the world is full of opportunities for creation, exploration, and growth. Inward, the soul whispers its deepest longings, often drowned out by fear or doubt. The Fool calls us to listen—to honor the leap not as an impulsive act but as an alignment with our authentic call.

Each leap reshapes us. Each step into the unknown reveals aspects of our being that cannot emerge in safety. Only by moving beyond the familiar do we discover the vastness of our capacity. The Fool is not a fool because they are ignorant; they are a fool because they trust.

And so, as you close these pages, you are invited not into finality but into beginning. The journey of Tarot does not end with *The World*; it begins again with the Fool. The circle completes only to open again, deeper and wider.

Where does your soul ask you to leap? Into what mystery are you being called? Where does wonder still shimmer on your horizon?

The Eternal Fool does not promise answers but offers companionship. With arms wide and eyes lifted, the Fool reminds us that every ending births a new beginning, every closure conceals an opening, every completion is but another step into the infinite unfolding of the soul.

So take a breath. Feel the invitation of the unknown. Trust that the leap, however uncertain, will carry you where you are meant to go. And as you step forward, know that the Fool walks beside you—always, forever, eternal.

Integrative Reflection

To conclude, let us integrate what has been revealed:

- **The Fool's Wonder** – Life is not meant to be fully understood but fully lived. Wonder is not naïveté; it is the courage to remain open in a world that tempts us toward cynicism.

- **The Fool's Risk** – Every step forward involves risk, whether of failure, rejection, or loss. Yet risk is the doorway to transformation. To live without risk is to live half-alive.

- **The Fool's Discovery** – What we find when we leap is rarely what we expect. The discovery is not in the outcome but in the expansion of selfhood that comes through the journey.

- **Tarot's Companionship** – The cards serve not as dictators of fate but as mirrors of truth. They are lifelong allies in reminding us who we are and who we are becoming.

- **The Next Leap** – Ultimately, the question is personal. No book, teacher, or oracle can tell you exactly where to go. The leap arises from within, and only you can hear its call.

This is the eternal invitation: *to leap again, and again, and again.*

Closing Meditation: Becoming the Fool

To ground these reflections, I invite you into a final meditation.

Close your eyes. Imagine yourself standing at the edge of a cliff. The sun is rising, bathing the horizon in gold. In your hand, you carry a small bundle—the sum of your experiences, lessons, and dreams. At your feet, a loyal companion waits, tail wagging, urging you onward.

Behind you lies the path already walked: the Magician's power, the Hermit's wisdom, the Tower's upheaval, the Star's hope, the World's completion. Each step has shaped you. Each card lives within you.

Now, before you lies the unknown. The Fool's call is clear: "Leap."

Do you trust the ground that will rise to meet you? Do you trust the wings of spirit to carry you? Do you trust your own soul to guide you?

Take a breath. Smile at the horizon. And step forward.

You are the Fool, eternal and infinite. Your path does not end here. It begins anew.

Benediction of the Eternal Fool

I walk with empty hands,
yet carry all I need.
I step into the unknown,
where mystery plants its seed.

The road behind has shaped me,
the stars above still shine,
Each ending is beginning,
each moment is divine.

Do not fear the leap,
for wings are always near,
The heart was made for wonder,
the soul was made to hear.

So onward into silence,
into song, into the skies,
The Fool is ever with you,
with laughter in their eyes.

About the Author

Arwin M. Valencia, MD, walks two worlds, one grounded in the precision of science, the other attuned to the mysteries of spirit. As a pediatrician and neonatologist, he has stood at the threshold of life countless times, bearing witness to the first fragile breaths of newborns and the sacred silence that sometimes follows. His professional journey, from his medical training at the **University of Santo Tomas**, through residency at **Richmond University Medical Center**, to fellowship at **UC Irvine**, has been shaped by both discipline and devotion. His academic contributions in neonatal research, including the microbiome, growth, and neurodevelopment, reflect a lifelong dedication to understanding the miracle of human life.

Yet medicine, for all its rigor, could not quiet the deeper questions of the soul. The experiences of birth and loss awakened in him an awareness that life's most profound truths are not measured by monitors or revealed through data alone. They emerge in silence, in mystery, and in the spaces where science ends and spirit begins. It was here that Dr. Valencia discovered the Tarot, not as superstition, but as a symbolic mirror of the psyche and a sacred map of the soul's journey.

In *Walking the Fool's Path*, he brings the Fool to life not as a jester, but as the eternal seeker, a soul who dares to leap into the unknown, trusting that each step, whether joyous or painful, is part of a greater unfolding. For Dr. Valencia, the Fool's journey is not an escape from reality, but a return to it, an invitation to rediscover innocence, embrace transformation, and awaken to the infinite within.

Writing both under his name and the pen name **MysticSojourn66**, he merges the insights of Jungian psychology, astrology, numerology, and quantum mysticism with his lived experience as physician and contemplative. His works form a bridge between worlds: where science meets spirit, where intellect bows to intuition, and where the individual soul remembers its belonging to the greater whole.

Through his writings, Dr. Valencia invites fellow seekers to walk beside him, to embrace the paradoxes of life, to find meaning in mystery, and to see each ending as the beginning of a new cycle. Like the newborns he has devoted his life to, every soul is forever beginning again, stepping into light with courage and wonder.

For him, the Fool is the eternal companion: the archetype that whispers, *"Leap, and you will be carried."* It is this spirit, bold, open-hearted, and infinitely curious, that animates both his healing work and his writing.